2012

The Myth of the Mayan Calendar

Also by August Noble

Semitopia

Copyright © MMIV August Noble.

All rights reserved. No part of this publication may be reproduced, stored in a retrieval system, or transmitted in any form or by any means, electronic, mechanical, recording or otherwise, without the prior written permission of August Noble.

2012

The Myth of the Mayan Calendar

By August Noble

2012
Debunking the
Myth of the Mayan Calendar

Using
Synchronicities
to
Discover Your Life's Mission

Healing the Planetary Consciousness
Through
Meditation and A P K

1

"So, how's it going, Mister Omega? You over your fear of flying, yet?" Diva Diamond asked, standing in the aisle of her private jet, her hand resting on the back of the seat to steady herself.

Alpha looked up from his yellow legal pad. The vision before him was a remarkable transformation. She had changed into jeans and a baggy sweatshirt, let her hair down, and removed her make-up and ten-inch nails. He smiled. "You changed your hair," he said.

She smirked. "That was a wig."

"And you took all that tinsel off your face."

She laughed, a high-pitched squeal that came from the depths of her soul. "No one ever called it that before. You're funny."

She lowered herself into the seat next to him and sank down into the plush material. The expansive reclining chair was larger and more luxurious than in most homes. "I just wanted to get comfortable. Let my wig down, if you know what I mean."

She gazed out into the night at the expanse of stars. Without turning her head from the window, she said, "You're a smart guy… how many stars are there?"

He shrugged his shoulders. "Billions and billions."

She continued looking out. "Which one is the brightest?"

"That all depends on your perspective; the closer you are, the brighter it appears."

"That's what I thought." She pushed a button and the electronic shutter drew the shade over the window. She turned her head toward

Alpha. "The only time I can relax is behind closed doors. I'm always on stage. Whenever I go out, all the paparazzi are clicking their cameras, just trying to get a compromising picture of me. Here, I can just be myself."

"I like it," he said. "You look nice."

She wriggled her nose. "You making a pass at me?"

He shook his head. "Can't an old man even compliment a pretty young lady without appearing to be a dirty old man?"

"All the dirty old men I know *are* dirty old men," she said sarcastically.

"I just meant that you looked…" he struggled for the right word. "…normal."

"I don't want to look *normal*. I'm a star; I'm not supposed to look normal. If I looked normal, I wouldn't be a star."

"Relax," he said. "You're not my type."

She tweaked his nose playfully. "Honey, don't kid yourself; I'm everyone's type."

He held out his left hand and displayed his wedding band. "I'm married; remember?"

"But, your wife is…" she started, but hesitated, not wanting to open an old wound. "All this time, and you still wear your wedding ring?"

He eyed her quizzically. "Why would I take it off?"

She thought. "Right." She changed the subject. "You want something to eat?"

"No thanks; I'm fine."

"Well, I'm hungry." She snapped her fingers.

Instantly, from out of nowhere, one of her assistants appeared, as if by magic.

"Gum," Diva demanded, holding out her hand, palm up.

Her assistant handed her a stick of gum.

Diva waved her hand in a dismissive gesture. "Gone."

Her assistant disappeared, vanishing back into nowhere.

Diva ripped the stick of gum in half. "Want to share this?" she asked Alpha, holding the piece out toward him. "I never chew a whole stick of gum. Too many calories."

"No thanks," he said.

"Suit yourself." She tossed it on the floor. She opened the other piece, stuck it in her mouth, tossed the wrapper into the aisle.

"I'm surprised you didn't have her unwrap it for you," he said, not altogether facetiously.

"Germs."

"Oh." He nodded. Eyed her. "That's all you're having for dinner?"

"I'm a superstar; I can't afford to get fat." She took the pad from his hands, glanced at the chicken scratch. "What are you writing? Two-oh-one-two," she read the large numbers emblazoned across the top of the page. That was all she could make out. She dropped it back in his lap. "And I thought my writing was bad."

He chuckled. "No one has to read it but me. I'll type it up as soon as I get back."

"Another book?" she asked.

He nodded.

"What's this one about?"

"The Mayan calendar. Have you heard about it?"

"Sure. Everybody's heard about it. Can't say I know much about it, though."

"What you just read. The year two thousand twelve. Supposedly, when the Mayan calendar runs out, the world will end."

She shook her head derisively. "I should have known. What is it about you and the end of the world?" She lowered her voice and said in a deep vibrato, "The end is near." She chuckled and gave his shoulder a friendly shove. "Lighten up, will you?"

"That's just the point; the end is not near," he scoffed. "The end of the Mayan calendar is nothing more than an urban myth. As a matter of fact…" He stopped abruptly. "You have to forgive me; I have a habit of launching into lecture mode. Old habits die hard."

"Go right ahead. I was going to take a sleeping pill, but a boring lecture will probably do as well." She folded her arms and looked up at the ceiling of the cabin. "In high school, I slept through every class."

"How did you manage to get away with that?"

"I wore dark glasses."

"And the teachers didn't object?"

"No way. They like students who are well-behaved. It makes their job easier. Teachers are nothing more than glorified baby sitters."

"I think I've just been insulted."

"Not at all. Someone has to do it."

"But, how did you get away with wearing sunglasses? Didn't the teachers know you were sleeping behind them?"

"No way. Teachers are clueless; they thought I was on drugs."

"Oh."

She closed her eyes. "Go ahead, tell me all about it; I'm all ears."

He intertwined his fingers and rested his hands on his notepad, debating with himself. On the one hand, sitting there, eyes closed, she did not appear to be all that attentive. But, on the other hand, no professor worth his salt had ever refused a captive audience.

"As you know," he started, "I have been teaching philosophy practically all my life, ancient literature mostly, primarily Biblical prophecy - the Book of Revelation, the Book of Daniel, the minor prophets from the Old Testament. Well, longs-story-short, in the past few years, I began getting more and more questions from my students concerning the ancient Mayan prophecies and the end of the Mayan calendar in 2012. Since it was outside my area of expertise, I decided to conduct a thorough research of the topic.

"I set out to find out everything the Maya had to say about the 2012 end-date. I wanted to consult the primary source documents, to see what the Maya actually said. To go straight to the horse's mouth, so to speak. I did not want to rely on translations or interpretations of secondary source material. I read everything I could lay my hands on.

"What I expected to find were manuscripts written by the Maya concerning the subject matter, but, while I discovered numerous reference works by British, American, and European scholars, much to my chagrin, I was unable to lay my hands on a single solitary volume written by an honest-to-goodness bona fide Mayan native.

"As it turned out, there was a good reason for the dearth of information. Nearly all of the ancient Mayan literature was destroyed in the Spanish Inquisition of 1562 by Father Diego de Landa. He declared that the Maya were heathens and that their books were superstition and lies of the Devil, and he ordered every last one of them burned. Only a handful of volumes managed to escape the flames."

"What a loss," she muttered.

He agreed. So, she is listening, after all, he thought, and continued where he had left off. "When I first discovered that fact, it was like the wind was knocked out of my sails. Even now, when I think of it, I have the same reaction as I do about the fire of the Library of Alexandria that consumed all the ancient Egyptian texts. All that information, vanished. The great secrets of an entire civilization, lost and gone forever."

"Why would people do such horrid things?"

"Why do people do anything they do?"

She voiced agreement. "Right. Go figure."

"At any rate," he went on, "I discovered that there were some books about ancient Maya lore, for instance, the *Popul Vuh*..."

"The what?" she interrupted him.

"The *Popol Vuh*. Literally, it means the *Book of the People* or the *Book of the Community* or *Book of the Council*, depending on how you want to translate the word. That, and *The Book of Chilam Balam*. Chilam Balam was an ancient Mayan prophet, on the order of our Moses," he offered by way of explanation, before she could interrupt him again and derail his train of thought. "I obtained copies of the original manuscripts. The first thing I noticed, right off the bat, was that they were not written in ancient Mayan hieroglyphics; they were in Spanish and Latin. Now, why, I asked myself, would the Maya write books in Spanish and Latin?"

"And what did yourself tell yourself?" she chimed in.

"The simple fact of the matter is, they were not written by the Maya at all; they were transcribed from Mayan oral tradition by the Spanish priests. And therein lies the key to the end-date myth."

"Huh? You lost me."

He pondered for a moment. "Let me give you an example. You have heard, no doubt, of the phrases, *in the beginning was the void*, and *let there be light*, and *then came the word*?"

"Sure. From the *Bible*."

"Wrong. Those particular phrases I just quoted come directly from the *Popol Vuh*. When I first read it, I was astounded by the uncanny similarities between the Mayan manuscripts and our own *Bible*. And then, I realized the reason why there were so many striking parallels. The Spanish priests were on a mission from God to convert the indigenous populations. What they created, weaving Mayan oral tradition around Christian doctrine, was nothing more than religious propaganda, designed to show the natives how closely their own holy books resembled the Christian *Bible*. So, since they were so similar in nature and content, the Maya would actually not be giving up their own religious beliefs by converting to Christianity. The *Book of Chilam Balam* contains numerous illusions to end-time prophecies and Armageddon-like scenarios; as a matter of fact, it reads like a Mayanized version of *The Book of Revelation*.

"Thus began the Mayan myths. But the myths are not myths *of* the Maya; they are, instead, myths *about* the Maya. And the biggest myth of all is that the world is going to end in 2012. I've read every book on the subject, studied every reference work, scrutinized every photograph, and I can state, categorically, that there is *no* Mayan passage anywhere that says that the world will end in 2012 - not on any Mayan manuscript, not on any Mayan monument, or temple, or tomb, or ruin, or stele, or sarcophagus, or pottery shard. None, zip, zilch, nada. It doesn't exist. It's all a myth, just an urban legend. The Maya themselves don't even believe it. Here, I'll show you. I have proof positive."

He reached down by his feet and grabbed his briefcase. He rested it on his knees, opened it, thumbed through the files and produced a document. "Case in point. You see this? This is a letter published in the memoirs of J. Eric Thompson."

"Who?"

"He was a British archeologist, one of the chief proponents of the 2012 end-date. I'll get to him in a bit, but first, I want you to see this."

She waved her hand in the air. "I'm resting my eyes. Just tell me what it says. I trust you."

He glanced at her, then read. "I'll just give you the pertinent information. Anyway, at any rate, here's the long and the short of it. In 1935, a lunar eclipse was witnessed in the Yucatan. A Mayan native who had worked for Thompson in Belize sent him a frantic letter, wanting to know if the eclipse portended the end of the world. This is what he wrote:

On the night of the 15th-16th of this month an eclipse of the moon was seen. All the people were frightened, saying the world would end that night. A lot of noise was made beating tin cans, boxes and bells. [There were] prayers and processions in the night at one o'clock. All were awake [believing] that was the moment of the [last] judgement.

"There you have it."

"There you have what?"

"The smoking gun that proves that not even the Maya believe in the 2012 end-date."

She opened her eyelids and peered at him directly with her deep piercing eyes. "All that says is that they were frightened by an eclipse.

That's understandable. A primitive people were frightened of an eclipse. So what does that prove?" She snapped her gum.

"You have to read between the lines. Why were they out in force banging their pots and pans?"

"I told you; because they were terrified of the eclipse," she huffed. "To ward off evil spirits, I suppose."

"Right. But why were they terrified of the eclipse?"

"Because they thought it was an omen of the end of the world."

"Exactly my point. Let's apply a little CSL."

"Huh? You lost me again."

"Oh. Sorry. *CSL.* I coined that phrase. Rather proud of it; clever of me if I do say so myself. It stands for *Common Sense Logic.* You see, there's all kinds of logic - you have your formal logic and your abstract logic and your mathematical logic and your symbolic logic and your scientific logic, that philosophers and mathematicians employ, but the one logic they always overlook is the simplest logic of all, the logical logic, the Common Sense Logic. This letter is the smoking gun that proves that not even the modern Maya believe in the 2012 end-date."

"Huh?"

"You have to read between the lines. Look at what he wrote. He said *all* the people were frightened that the world would end that night. *All* were awake. He did not say *some* were frightened, or *several*, or even a *few*. He said *all*; *all* of the people were frightened. That proves that it was not just a few of the Maya who held that fear; it was the general consensus of the Maya that the world would end that very night.

"Now, applying Common Sense Logic, why would they be concerned about an eclipse in 1935 if they actually believed that the Apocalypse was not going to come until 2012? The sixty-four thousand dollar question is, why would they be afraid that the world would end that night if they knew that the world still had another seventy-seven years to go?"

She pulled on her lower lip. "You're right; that is a good question."

He clapped his hands. "And there can only be one answer. And the answer is that the Maya do not believe that the world is going to end in 2012. That is purely an invention cut from the whole cloth of the Western fertile imagination, steeped in end-times Biblical lore, lifted right out of *The Book of Revelation*. So, if the Maya do not believe the 2012 prediction, then why should we?"

"Good point. You certainly convinced me."

"If only it were that simple to convince everyone. What I had discovered was, there was no truth to it whatsoever; it was nothing more than an urban legend. But, for whatever reason, it simply refused to go away. Even when I proved that 2012 was not a myth that the Maya subscribed to, I continued to get questions concerning it from my students. I began to wonder why otherwise bright intelligent logical students would be taken in by what was so obviously a total and complete hoax. And that led me to a deeper inquiry into the nature of belief itself, because the whole 2012 end-date hinges on what we believe and why we choose to believe it."

He studied her closely. Her eyes were closed. "You asleep?"

She did not open her eyes, but she flashed a broad grin and snapped her gum. "No, I'm awake." She chuckled.

"What's so funny?"

"You just reminded me of an old joke from when I was a kid: *What's the one question you can never answer 'yes' to?*"

He thought. "I give up."

"Are you asleep?"

He laughed. "That's a good one."

"Go on, she said. "I'm listening. Don't worry; I'll tell you when I fall asleep."

He laughed again. Then, he scratched his chin. "Let me see, where was I?"

"You were talking about *beliefs*."

She had been absorbing his lecture, he thought. Apparently, paying more attention to it than he had. He revved up his mental engine and started again. "Well, as I was saying, I began to question the very nature of belief and why we believe what we do. In order to understand the 2012 end-of-the-world myth, it is necessary to first understand the very nature of belief and the psychology of the urban legend. Consider this about our beliefs system: two thousand years ago, in Jerusalem, a small band of zealots firmly believed that Jesus of Nazareth was the Messiah. On the other hand, there were those who chose not to believe. In other words, given the exact same information, some chose to believe, and some chose not to believe. They all had the same data, the same information, the same evidence. And yet, the different groups held, at that time, and even to this day, widely disparate beliefs.

"Now, fast forward to today. Many are just as firm believers and many are just as firm non-believers. If people could be swayed by evidence, then one would expect that they would all be believers or non-believers. And still, there are *believing* Christians, and *non-believing* Jews. As well as non-believing Moslems, Hindus, Buddhists, Confucians, Taoists, and yes, even *non-believing* atheists. After two millennia of debating the evidence, each side refuses to be convinced of the other's viewpoint. And not only that, but, using the identical database of information, i.e., the *Bible*, there are a myriad of Christian denominations, with new sects and cults being added every day, who staunchly and firmly believe that their religion is the correct, and only, correct *one*. Even as a child, I often wondered, if all Christians believe in the same *Bible*, then how is it possible to have different denominations? And if one set of data is true, then how is it possible to have different religions?

"On a secular level, consider a court of law. Twelve jurors, hearing the same evidence, can come to startlingly different conclusions, some believing, beyond the shadow of a doubt that the defendant is innocent, while others believing, just as firmly, beyond the shadow of a doubt, that the defendant is guilty. We choose to believe what we choose to believe. By the same token, opinion polls can cite polar opposite opinions across the spectrum. But, in the final analysis, that is all it is - an opinion.

"Urban legends abound in our culture. To put it in simple terms, an urban legend is something that we take to be true, but is not true. They are myths that have permeated our mass consciousness so thoroughly that we no longer even doubt their veracity.

"In the category of urban legends, our folk heroes and historical figures are ripe for the picking. Take, for instance, Davy Crockett. Does anyone doubt that he killed a bear when he was only three?"

"Well, it was easier than killing a fully-grown bear," she quipped.

He laughed, then continued. "George Washington, father of our country, is yet another case in point. Does anyone question whether or not George Washington actually tossed a silver dollar across the river?"

"Just another example of big government throwing our money away."

"Then, too, can you believe all the plaques claiming *George Washington slept here*?"

She snapped her gum. "Apparently, he ready did sleep around. Maybe that's why he's called the *Father Of Our Country*."

He grinned. "But then, if he did commit such an infamous deed, one can be absolutely certain that he would have owned up to his transgression, as he so clearly demonstrated when he turned state's evidence after chopping down the cherry tree, professing…"

"*I cannot tell a lie,*" she chimed in.

"I thought you said you slept through high school."

"Only the boring parts."

"Well, I'm glad to see that I'm not boring you."

She make a fake snoring sound. "Carry on. Fire away."

He smiled. "One of the most famous examples of an urban legend that exists even to this day, involves a young couple parked in a cemetery at night."

"Wait a minute. Why would they be parked in a cemetery?"

"Because, it's romantic."

"Not at night, it isn't."

He sighed deeply. "Okay then, we'll say that they were parked on lovers' lane."

"That's better. By the way, where is lovers' lane, anyhow?"

"In the cemetery."

She groaned.

"As the story goes, they hear a report on the radio that a homicidal maniac has escaped from an insane asylum and is on the lose, in search of his next victim. He could be easily spotted, since he had a hook for a hand.

"Scared out of their wits by the news, the couple immediately drives away at a high rate of speed. When she opens her car door, the hook is on her door handle!"

"Wait a minute, why didn't he find the hook?"

"Because it was on her door."

"But why didn't he come around and open the door for her? He wasn't much of a gentleman, if you ask me."

"Okay, I misspoke. Let me rephrase it. Being the gentlemanly knight in shining armor that he was, he got out of the car, walked around to her side, and discovered the hook on her door handle. Is that better?"

"Much. That's enough to send chills racing up and down the spine of any red-blooded suitor. Did he ask her out on a second date?"

"I don't know. You're missing the point."

"What is the point? That a homicidal maniac ruined a perfectly good evening for them?"

He heaved a huge sigh, bowed his head in desperation, and then and only then, when he glanced over at her and saw her broad grin, did he realize that she had been teasing him the whole time. "You had me going," he said, frowning.

"And you fell for it, hook, line, and sinker," she snickered. "Get it? Hook. Line and sinker. Get it?" She giggled uproariously, thoroughly enjoying her little pun.

He nodded. And smiled. "Yes; I get."

She shoved his shoulder playfully. "You're too easy. I was just pulling your leg. Go on; finish your story; don't let me stop you."

He sat silent, eyes glazed over.

She sat up. Checked him out. "What's the matter?" she asked. "I hurt your feelings?"

"No. Not at all. It's just that, when you laugh, you remind me of..." He did not finish the sentence.

She finished it in her mind. She rubbed his shoulder. "You're still not over it?"

"Some things, you never get over." He turned toward her. "It leaves one with half a heart."

She rubbed his arm. "I'm sorry I interrupted your story. Go on. I really am interested in hearing this." She settled back again.

He managed a wan smile and continued. "That story contains what appears to be, at least on the surface, a kernel of truth, so at that level, it is believable, while at the same time, it has more than a full measure of nail-biting, gut-wrenching, spine-tingling horror. And that presents the other component that is so tantalizingly seductive about the urban legend: the element of horror, of fear, of deep dark jeopardy.

"Consider another urban legend, this one having a more modern ring to it, but still bearing the semblance of plausibility. A woman was washing her cat. Apparently short of towels, she placed the cat in the microwave oven to dry. What supposedly happened next is better left to the imagination."

"Ouch!" She scrunched up her face like she had just bitten into a sour pickle. "Don't tell me; let me guess. Cat kabob?"

He nodded sadly. "Only thing is, it never happened. Both of those urban legends have crept into the collective consciousness, and many people believe that they are true. The only problem is, neither of them bear an ounce of veracity. In the first instance, no man with a hook ever escaped from an insane asylum to wreak havoc on an unsuspecting populace. If he had, one can be certain that it would have been on the front page of every newspaper in the country. It never was, because it never happened."

"And the case of the nuked cat?"

He shook his head slowly from side to side. "If that episode had ever really occurred, you know what would have happened?"

"The animal lovers' society would have been all over it like white on rice?"

He chuckled. "You got that right. And yet, the fact of the matter remains, no one has ever been arrested for the crime, no one has ever been prosecuted, or convicted, or sentenced, or incarcerated for what can only be described as an egregiously heinous offense."

"And yet, people believe that they're true?" It was a question and a statement.

"Right. Urban legends have become so deeply ingrained in the collective psyche that they are not even given any thought. When queried, most people will affirm that they do not subscribe to any fallacy; that they only believe the truth, the whole truth, and nothing but the truth. But, consider the following: what does a cracked mirror mean?"

"That's easy; seven years' bad luck."

"How about this one? A black cat crosses your path."

"A bad omen."

"Step on a crack…?"

"Break your mother's back."

"See? And you said you don't believe in urban legends."

"That's different; those are superstitions. They aren't legends; they just are."

"Exactly. And that's what makes urban legends so insidious. They enter our consciousness so stealthily that the average person doesn't even realize that they are there, lurking behind the frontal lobe, just waiting to pounce on the unsuspecting victim.

"For instance, in what movie did Humphrey Bogart say *Play it Again, Sam*?"

"That's easy; *Casablanca*."

"That's what most people would say. The fact of the matter is, Humphrey Bogart never said *Play it again, Sam*. The line he delivered was simply, *Play it, Sam*, but when asked what Bogie said, the majority of people will insert that little, but significant word, *again*."

"That's nit-picking."

"No; that's splitting hairs, but let me give you another test: in the original 1931 version of the movie, *Frankenstein*, who played Frankenstein?"

"*Boris Karloff*."

"That's what the majority of people would say. But, in actuality, Boris Karloff played *The Monster*. Doctor Henry Frankenstein, the mad scientist, was played by Colin Clive; his father, Baron Frankenstein, was played by Frederick Kerr. But, show anyone a picture of the anvil-headed, electrode-necked monster, and ask them who it is, and they will immediately reply *Frankenstein*."

"Okay, I'll grant you that, but what's the point?"

"Only this: for whatever reason, people would rather believe a fable than the truth. I guess it's just human nature. When people have the choice between believing a lie and the truth, they will pick the lie every time. For instance, when Christopher Columbus tried to embark on his voyage to find a short-cut to the West Indies it took him thirteen years to raise the money because people believed that the earth was flat, even though the other celestial objects in the sky, the sun and the moon are clearly round, and during a lunar eclipse, one can plainly see the circular outline of the earth's shadow on the moon. They wouldn't believe the evidence of their own eyes.

"And Galileo was placed under house arrest and spent the last decade of his life in virtual captivity because he proclaimed that the Sun, and not the Earth, was the center of our solar system. All down through history, people have been more willing to believe the lie than the truth. It's gotten to the point where I would take the consensus opinion and then vote in the opposite direction, because, more often than not, the majority opinion is wrong.

"I've noticed the same thing with gossip. The tabloids print such godawful things about me, and people just eat it up as though it were the gospel truth. Why do you think that is?"

"Perhaps it is because our lives lack drama. The human animal craves excitement. That is why there are roller coaster rides and scary movies. We love to be thrilled and chilled, to escape from the humdrum existence of everyday life. In the words of Henry David Thoreau, *the mass of men lead lives of quiet desperation*. Fact may be stranger that fiction, but the fiction makes far more interesting reading.

"The end of the Mayan calendar is no exception. It is based on a modicum of truth that sounds plausible enough on the surface, but is so far removed from our modern-day culture that its verification remains problematic. Add to that the allure of the fantastic, the mystical, not to mention the most horrific event of all time - the end of the world, and you have all the makings of the classic urban legend."

He adjusted himself on his chair to be able to better face her. "We tend to put credence in things that are mysterious and mystical. The fact of the matter is, the average person knows so little about the Maya that it is easy to ascribe arcane knowledge to the Maya that they did not actually possess. Let us apply Common Sense Logic. The whole idea behind the 2012 myth is that the Maya were such astute prognosticators that they could predict, thousands of years in advance, the end of our world. But, if they were so wise, then where are they today? Why did their civilization die out? Why were they unable to foretell their own future? Why did they not see their conquest by the Aztecs, or the

Toltecs, or the Spanish? At fortune-telling, they had a dismal track record. We are placing our collective fate in the hands of an ancient society that was not able to sustain their own culture, and we are attributing advanced knowledge to a people who were not even able to invent the wheel."

"So, where did the legend come from? Where did it start?" she asked.

"Actually, from a series of synchronicities."

"Synchronicities?"

"Coincidences that really aren't coincidences."

"Oh, sure, I know what you mean. They happen to me all the time."

"Actually this story absolutely abounds with synchronicities, but I'll get into that later; first, let's start with J.T. Goodman. He was the man who originally claimed to have cracked the Mayan calendar. The synchronicities start there, but they certainly don't end there. Goodman was the owner of a newspaper in the Nevada Territory, in Virginia City, called *The Territorial Enterprise*. An interesting synchronicity is that he gave Mark Twain his first job as a reporter."

"Twain. I've heard of him."

"I knew you didn't sleep through all your classes."

"Maybe I absorbed it during my sleep."

"Through osmosis?"

"Who? Donny Osmond?"

He sighed. "Yeah. That's right."

She looked puzzled. "I don't get it. How could Donny Osmond…?"

He cut her off. "If you'll just listen, I'll explain it to you." Then, adroitly, he changed the subject. "In order to understand how the 2012 urban legend was perpetuated, one has to understand the psychological make-up of the men who concocted it. J.T. Goodman, that is, Joseph T. Goodman, born 1838, died 1917, was a rascal, a rapscallion, a shyster, a scalawag, a charlatan. You name it, he was it. The original con man. He would do anything for a buck. Not to mention which, he also happened to be a poet, a playwright, a short-story writer, and an author of what would today be called *romance novels* and *Western adventures.*

"At any rate, he tried a lot of different occupations, from gold and silver prospector to raisin raiser."

"He raised raisins? I never heard of that."

"Actually grapes."

"Oh, so that's where they come from."

"Anyway, all the time he was trying his hand at a variety of disparate occupations, he was writing all of his various and assorted pieces of fiction. Unable to place any of his stories with any publisher, he decided to do the next best thing. While prospecting in the Nevada Territory, unsuccessfully, I might note, a newspaper came up for sale. Goodman alighted upon a brilliant idea. If no one else would publish his stories, he would publish them himself, in his own newspaper. In the days before television or motion pictures or radio or even the telephone, the major entertainment was the local newspaper. Many writers got their start in the publishing world by serializing their novels. Such notables as Charles Dickens and Arthur Conan Doyle made it a time-honored tradition. If it was good enough for them, then it was certainly good enough for him, and Goodman decided to follow in their footsteps. He and a friend, Denis E. McCarthy, purchased the bankrupt newspaper, and as they say, the rest is history.

"Their newspaper, *The Territorial Enterprise,* became the purveyor of the most outlandish fabrications ever set in type. Goodman, as owner-editor, played fast and loose with the facts. Nothing was too preposterous for him to print. In the process, he had invented the first tabloid newspaper. Mark Twain once said of him, *After Goodman had his way with a story, the truth could not be located with a divining rod.* But, Goodman had struck upon the winning combination. He loved telling tall tales and the public loved reading them. Before long, his newspaper was the largest-circulation paper in the entire West.

"Unfortunately, their questionable style of reporting was not without its disadvantages. Constantly overstepping the boundaries of honesty and decorum, the reporters were constantly up to their necks in hot water, as well as lawsuits. In order to protect themselves from the wrath of incensed readers, the reporters changed their names to protect the guilty, assuming noms de plume. William Wright became Dan DeQuille. James William Emery Townsend was known as *Lying Jim*. Samuel Langhorne Clemens became Mark Twain. Mark Twain, incidentally, after being challenged to one duel too many, high-tailed it out of town, *three steps ahead of the undertaker* as he put it in his autobiography, *Roughing It*.

"Twain was not the only reporter who tired of the backlash that the yellow journalism generated. Goodman's other employees also eventually left for greener pastures, creating a revolving door for cub reporters who wanted to get their feet wet in the publishing waters. Even Denis McCarthy, Goodman's original partner and co-owner of *The Territorial Enterprise*, found its dubious editorial policies not entirely to his liking, sold his share and purchased *The Virginia Evening Chronicle*, a rival newspaper, which he ran as a legitimate newspaper until his death in 1885.

"*The Territorial Enterprise* also came under fire for the practice of what today would be called *pump and dump* schemes. They would buy stock in a mining company, then print a report in their newspaper that that particular mining company had struck a rich vein of ore. When the stock price soared, they would sell off their shares, at a healthy profit, which they would then promptly squander at the gambling tables in the local saloons. The had a not altogether undeserved reputation for spending their money as fast, and oftentimes faster, than they could earn it. One could add profligate gambler and bon vivant to their laundry list of stellar character traits.

"One such stock scheme involved the *Bonanza Kings*, owners of the Comstock Lode claims, who, thanks in no small part, to the exaggerated stories printed in *The Territorial Enterprise,* turned an initial investment of seventy-five thousand dollar in stocks into a tidy profit of over a hundred million dollars, when speculators drove the price of the shares up to eight hundred dollars apiece. An enormous sum even by today's standards, it was astronomical for the times, in an era when people worked twelve hour days for a dollar a day, mind you. As a direct result of their stock manipulations, the SEC was established."

"Sex?"

"Not *S E X*; *S E C*; the *Securities and Exchange Commission*."

"Oh."

"But, that was another synchronicity, and we'll get back to it in a minute. But, back to Goodman. Being a newspaper man, he met virtually anyone and everyone who was anyone, especially if they had a sensational story that he could print. One such individual was none other than Dr. Gustavus Eisen, the eminent Mayan archeologist. In the 1800's, the discovery of ancient Mayan ruins had captured the popular imagination. When Dr. Eisen confided to Goodman that he and his partner, the renowned English Mayan archeologist, Alfred Maudslay, were seeking an editor for their new volume, *The Archaic Maya Inscriptions,* Goodman immediately offered his services."

"I don't get it; where's the synchronicity in that?"

"If Goodman had not have been a newspaperman, he would never had met Dr. Eisen, and if he had not published a scandal rag, he probably would not have been all that interested in Mayan arcana, and thus, would not have even bothered to interview him. At any rate, J.T. Goodman caught a boat for England, where he assisted Maudslay in editing his book, one of his duties being to collate the numerous photographs found in the appendix of the book. Many of the photographs were of Mayan date inscriptions, and when Maudslay told Goodman that no one had been able to crack the Mayan calendar code, the latter saw the golden opportunity of a lifetime. The individual who solved the Mayan calendar riddle would be instantly famous, not to mention famously rich."

"What do you mean, crack the calendar code? Was it a secret, or something?" she asked.

"In a way, it was, but only because the Mayan calendar is completely different from the Gregorian calendar that we use. Remember that I told you that Father de Landa burned all the Mayan books in 1562?"

"Vaguely."

"Well, when he burned those manuscripts, he also eliminated any way to correlate the Mayan calendar with the Christian calendar. What was needed to compare the two was some common event that was recorded in the Mayan manuscripts, and dated, such as the arrival of Cortés. If the Maya did write about that, we will probably never know, because de Landa destroyed all the evidence. Armed with Maudslay's date inscription photographs and de Landa's diaries, Goodman set out to accomplish what Mayan scholars had been trying in vain for decades to do - date the Mayan calendar.

"One piece of information at his disposal was known as the Dresden Codex. As another synchronicity, this manuscript escaped destruction in de Landa's auto de fa because it was believed to be Aztec in origin. It eventually ended up in the Royal Saxon Library of Dresden, in the Aztec collection. When Ernst Forstemann assumed the job as director of the museum, he noticed that the hieroglyphics on the Dresden Codex did not resemble those on the other Aztec manuscripts. As synchronicity would have it, he saw some early Mayan ruin photographs that Maudslay had published in the *Biologia Centralia-Americana* series and realized that the Dresden Codex was not Aztec at all, but instead Mayan. He then set about the formidable task of translating the Dresden Codex, and after some fourteen years of arduous labor, he had deciphered the Mayan system of mathematics and determined that the Codex was a table of eclipses. At long last, there was a way to correlate the Christian and the Mayan calendars.

"J.T. Goodman toiled at the task for several years, without making much progress. After all, working with scant information, long before the advent of the computer, it was a daunting challenge. It had taken Ernst Forstemann fourteen years to decipher the Dresden Codex. By this time, Goodman was already in his sixties, in an age when many people did not live much beyond fifty. Realizing that, for him, time was running out, he made a momentous decision. He reasoned that, if he was unable to date the Mayan calendar, neither could anyone else. Up to that point, no one had been able to. He had no shortage of ego, and he figured if he was unable to do it, then no one else could, either. And if no one else could, then there would be no one who could refute whatever claim he made.

"The Mayan calendar actually consists of two separate parts: the long count date and the calendar round date. Roughly speaking, the long count corresponds to the year, while the calendar round, composed of the tzolkin, or the sacred calendar, and the haab, or the civil calendar, could be compared to the current month and day. The problem with dating the Mayan calendar is that after their classical period, the Maya abandoned the use of long count dates in their monument inscriptions. The only part that the modern Maya use today is the calendar round, which repeats itself every 52 years. And therein lies the problem. Knowing the calendar round date without knowing the long count date reveals nothing about the actual year date. It would be like going to a cemetery and seeing only half a date on a tombstone."

"Cemetery… ooh, that's gross."

"Well, maybe, but that's basically what the Mayan monuments were: headstones where their rulers were buried. Their monuments were mausoleums or graves."

She shivered slightly at the thought.

"Anyway, as I was saying, suppose you saw this date on a tombstone: *Monday, July Fourth.* What would the year be?"

"I don't know; I'd need a calendar to work it out."

"Coming right up." He reached into his briefcase and produced an almanac.

She laughed. "You carry an almanac in your brief case?"

"Doesn't everyone?"

"You carry everything in there. I bet you even have the kitchen sink in there."

"Let me see." He stuck his head into his brief case, pretending to look for a kitchen sink, then re-emerged. "Nope. I must have left it at home." He grinned.

She smiled.

He turned to the perpetual calendar. "See, here?"

She leaned over to get a better view.

"This is a perpetual calendar, good until the end of time."

"Forever and a day."

"Nope. Just until forever. After that, you're on your own."

Another hearty laugh.

He pointed to the page, running his finger across the columns. "If you know the day, Monday, July Fourth, the year could be 1966, 1977, 1983, 1994, or even 1825, for that matter. There's really no way of knowing, if you only have a partial date. That's what Goodman was up against. He had the current Mayan haab date, but not the long count. So, he had to turn to guess work. An inscription on Stele C at Quirigua…"

"Say what?"

"Quirigua. It's an ancient Mayan site in Guatemala. It depicts the setting in place of the three hearthstones. End-daters interpret this to be the creation of the Universe. There is a date at the top reading *4 Ahaw 8 Cumku*. Near the bottom is a glyph for *thirteen baktun*. Mayanists have theorized that that means the Mayan calendar will end when it reaches the thirteenth baktun."

"You lost me."

"A baktun is a Mayan time period of time, 144,000 days, actually. So, thirteen baktun is equivalent to 1,872,000 days, or 5,125 years. Mayanists call it a *great cycle*, or a *Mayan era* or *Mayan epoch*. Since Goodman knew the current haab date that the modern Maya were using, he extrapolated backwards. He reasoned that the end of the Mayan calendar would fall on the shortest day of the year, the winter solstice. Using a perpetual calendar, he determined when the closest winter solstice would work into the equation and came up with 2012. I always have to laugh when someone says that the Maya must have been bright to know when the solstice would fall, thousands of years hence. It wasn't the Maya at all who determined that; it was Goodman, who found that date and then worked backwards to the beginning of the Mayan calendar."

"So, it was all just guesswork."

"Pretty much so."

"Didn't anyone call him on it and raise a stink? How did he get away with it?"

"He had a couple of aces up his sleeve. Number one, at the time, no one else had been able to date the Mayan calendar, so no one could prove that he was wrong. And to make that job more difficult, he refused to reveal his equations during his lifetime, so none of his critics were given any ammunition to use against him. The other thing working in his favor was one of those synchronicities I mentioned before. Remember when I said that his newspaper, *The Territorial Enterprise*, was instrumental in making the *Bonanza Kings* immensely wealthy? Well one of those *Silver Kings* was none other than George Hearst."

"Say who?"

"George Hearst. The father of William Randolph Hearst, the newspaper magnate. George won the deed to the *San Francisco Examiner* in a card game. He gave the newspaper to his son, who used his father's immense fortune to acquire a chain of newspapers across the country, and in England. Besides newspapers, he also added a string of magazines to his collection, every important publication, from *Harper's Bazaar*, to *Cosmopolitan*, to *Good Housekeeping*, to *Town and Country*. At one point, he owned every major news outlet on the continent. Besides which, he published the *American Weekly*, which was inserted into every Hearst Sunday newspaper. His vast publishing empire allowed him to virtually control the dissemination of news.

"And that was how Goodman was able to pull it off. He had a lifetime of connections in the publishing world. Having been the owner-editor of the largest-circulation newspaper in the West, he had made a name for himself in his own right. He was the newspaperman's newspaperman, a celebrity of the printed word, if you will. And being an insider, he knew all the tricks of the trade. He knew how to generate headlines, how to create news, but most important of all, he knew how to shut out the competition. And using the influence of William Randolph Hearst, that was exactly what he did.

"Goodman traveled the country on an extended lecture tour, and needless to say, in every city that he visited, the local Hearst newspaper sang his praises. His arrival received front page banner headlines, as the genius who had solved the Mayan calendar mystery. His opponents didn't stand a chance of having their theories heard. If the opposing viewpoint received any press at all, it was relegated to the small type in the back of the newspaper.

"And with each story, the hyperbole and bombast escalated. The broadsides, which praised his achievements, while at the same time attacked his critics mercilessly, often bore bylines of unknown reporters, and were, in all probability, penned by Goodman himself."

"The constant bombardment of print adulation added greatly to his stature. The dilettante with no archeological credentials whatsoever proclaimed himself as the world's leading expert on Mayan antiquities. He was in great demand as a lecturer extraordinaire, a natural-born story-teller and raconteur. The man who had no university degree, no formal training, began billing himself *Professor Goodman* and later on, assumed the title of *Doctor Goodman*. It was an honorary title, to be sure, even though the honor was bestowed on himself by himself. But, his audiences did not care what he called himself. They were mesmerized by his fabricated tales of harrowing jungle adventures, accompanied by the photographs of Mayan ruins he claimed to have taken, which were, in fact, the work of the Alfred Maudslay. His reputation soared, to say nothing of his bank account. But the real bottom line was, as his fame and notoriety grew, so did the 2012 urban legend.

"In all likelihood, Goodman's erroneous dating of the Mayan calendar would have been forgotten and faded into the dim mists of history with his demise in 1917, had it not been for the arrival upon the scene of the next standard-bearer, J. Eric Thompson. Thompson, an Englishman, had tried his hand at various occupations, from sailor to World War One soldier to rancher in Argentina. While in South America, he was fascinated by the tales of ancient civilizations which circulated there. As synchronicity would have it, it was at that very time that the Carnegie Institution announced that it was launching its now famous *Chichén Itzá Project* of 1924. They put out a call for experts in the field of Mayan archeology to join their expedition into the hinterland of the Yucatan in search of lost civilizations.

"Thompson had, at long last, found his true calling. The allure of mysterious adventure, along with the added inducement of fame and glory, not to mention fortune, was too enticing to ignore."

"Fortune?"

"Treasure hunting was a lucrative business in those days. Thompson was an opportunist, a fortune hunter, and a quick way to turn a buck was by selling ancient artifacts to wealthy collectors."

"Artichokes?"

"Artifacts. Relics," he explained.

"Oh."

"He figured that if he could insinuate himself into the expedition, the world of ancient artifacts would be his oyster. The only problem was, he was not, by any means, a Mayan scholar. Without any university degrees to his name, he knew that it would be next to impossible to contend with the legitimate Mayanists competing for the coveted spots on the roster. What he needed was to find a way in the back door.

"He absorbed all of the available Mayan literature. One of the things he learned was that Goodman's death had created a vacuum, and a power struggle, of sorts, had erupted among certain Mayan archeologists vying for the position of Mayan calendrical expert for the expedition. A number of them had advanced their own calendar dating system, each of which was severely at odds with Goodman's 2012 end-date.

"It was also evident to Thompson that the Hearst news empire had been the champion of Goodman's cause. By supporting Goodman's 2012 hypothesis, Thompson knew that he would ingratiate himself with the newspaper mogul. Playing the political card, he presented himself to the Carnegie Institution as a Mayan calendar expert and a staunch supporter of Goodman's 2012 hypothesis.

"A number of Mayan calendar scholars had applied to the Carnegie Institution for the position, but the board of directors realized that if they took on anyone who was antithetical to the 2012 end-date, they would antagonize the powerful media mogul. That would cut off their access to the Hearst outlets, among which was the *Hearst Movietone News*, which provided newsreels to theaters across the nation. Since Thompson touted the 2012 end-date, they came to the decision that it behooved their cause to hire Thompson instead."

"So, it was all political."

"It was all political," he agreed. "But when you get right down to it, every decision is a political decision. In this case, they all benefited. It was a deal made in heaven. Thompson got his place on the Carnegie Chichén Itzá Project and access to ancient ruins; the Carnegie Institution got their publicity; and Hearst got exclusive rights to the stories."

"So, it was a conspiracy; they were all in cahoots."

"I don't know if you could call it a conspiracy as much as a case of *one hand washes the other - you scratch my back and I'll scratch yours*. The publicity that the Hearst machine provided ensured that the expeditions would be amply funded. By the same token, promoting Thompson in the Hearst press as the preeminent Mayan authority virtually guaranteed that he would be included in any Mayan expedition. At the same time, having an insider like Thompson assured Hearst of the choicest Mayan treasures. Many of them went directly into Hearst's private collection. Remember that Hearst owned the *Movietone News*. On the surface, it provided movie theatre newsreels, but it was also a thinly-veiled disguise for his collection operations.

"Hearst was an avid collector of anything and everything; the older, the better. His Movietone crews scoured the globe in search of stories, but news was not the only thing that they were searching for - they shipped back boatloads of antiques to Hearst's castle in San Simeon. Thompson provided Hearst with a steady stream of the best that the ancient Maya had to offer."

"So, basically, they stole them."

"Well, yes and no."

"How can it be yes or no? Either they did or they didn't; you can't have it both ways."

"In those days, the laws of treasure hunting were essentially that the treasures belonged to whomever found them. It was basically a case of finders keepers, losers weepers. But in the long run, it turned out that Thompson was the big loser. His fortune was assured, but he was a tortured unhappy soul."

"What did he have to be unhappy about? He got what he wanted, didn't he? He manipulated them into getting him on the expedition. His career was established. It sounds like he was sitting pretty."

"You know that old saying, *be careful what you wish for; you may get it?*"

"Tell me about it; it's the story of my life."

"And, as it turned out, Thompson's, too. His career was based on a lie, and it would perpetually haunt him.. By attaching himself to the 2012 hoax, he had painted himself into a corner. If it were ever decisively refuted, his entire life's work would come crashing down like a house of cards. He spent the rest of his life covering his tracks, going to any length to discredit his detractors. He often resorted to browbeating, name-calling, personal attacks, and character assassination.. He was a despicable wretched human being who destroyed the reputation and career of more than one individual. The way in which he demeaned his adversaries, and prevented them from receiving recognition for their accomplishments, bespeaks an angry, bitter human being.

"In the process, what he did was stifle legitimate Mayan scholarship. Upon Thompson's death, Michael Coe, whom Thompson referred to as *Fat Boy*, said that he had single-handedly set back Mayan scholarship by fifty years.

"Thompson had a long-running battle with the Russian archeologist, Yuri Valentinovich Knorosov. They were at odds over everything Mayan, but their biggest dispute was over the translation of the Mayan hieroglyphics. Thompson claimed to have deciphered their meaning, and even published several volumes describing them. He claimed that the Mayan language was idea-based; whereas Knorosov averred that they were phonetically-based. One must bear in mind that Thompson made his claims without ever learning to read a single Mayan language, and in fact, never even bothered to learn to speak the Mayan tongue. Knorosov, on the other hand, was an expert in Chinese, Japanese, and Egyptian glyphic writing systems. Thompson was able to keep him from publishing in any of the peer-reviewed archeology journals for some forty years, and effectively put the kibosh on Knorosov's prestige and thus, his career. But, the real losers, were us, the general public. We were deprived of authentic Mayan research, and the state of Mayan knowledge still suffers for it to this very day."

"So, who was right? Thompson or the Russian?"

"As it turned out, Knorosov was right all along. But that fact was not established until after Thompson's death relinquishing his domineering stranglehold on the field of study. In the meantime, his pig-headedness meant that half-a-century's worth of Mayan language research was completely worthless and had to be discarded. "

"So, Thompson was wrong again. Strike two."

"That's not all he was wrong about. He contended that the inscriptions on the Mayan monuments referred to their gods. That resulted in a long and heated debate that extended over decades. Now, it has been proved, beyond the shadow of a doubt, that the inscriptions depict the heroic feats of their leaders."

"So, Thompson didn't have much of a track record. He was oh for three."

"He was zero for everything. But the point is simply that Thompson was proved wrong about the translation of Mayan writing; he was proved wrong about the meaning of the Mayan inscriptions. So, why would anyone believe that he was right about the end of the Mayan calendar?"

"If you can't believe him about that, then you can't believe him about this."

"Right you are. He was completely wrong about the end of the Mayan calendar. As a matter of fact, it doesn't end at all. Any more than our calendar ends. That's the whole idea of the long count. It just goes on and on and on, as our does. The round count cycles. Just like a clock on the wall, it goes around and around and around. Now, when the hands on the clock get to twelve, the clock doesn't run out of time, and when the Mayan calendar round recycles after fifty-two years, it will just keep going merrily on its way, as it has for thousands of years in the past."

"Then, why did he say it ended?"

"Because, that makes it fascinating. And if it's fascinating, it's interesting. And if it's interesting, then it's lucrative."

"Ah, huh. The money motive rears its ugly head yet again. That's always behind it all. If you want to get to the truth, just follow the money."

"So it seems. By the way, remember when I mentioned before that this entire case was fraught with synchronicities?"

"Right."

"Well, there is another synchronicity between J.T. Goodman and Eric Thompson. The *T* in Goodman stands for Thompson."

"Ah." She smiled. "Cool."

"At any rate, by hitching his wagon to a falling star, Thompson was forever behind the eight ball. He was constantly on the defensive."

"You can run, but you can't hide."

"You got that right. The whole 2012 hypothesis was shot through and through with holes. For the rest of his life, Eric Thompson was like the little boy trying to plug the hole in the dyke. The moment he stopped up one leak, another one would erupt. It was as though for the rest of his career, he was engaged in damage control.

"The biggest problem that he had was that there simply is no Mayan calendar."

"There is no Mayan calendar?"

"Nope. None Nada. Zip. Zilch."

"But, you just said there was."

"No Mayan calendar has ever been found. No Mayan calendar, per se. Not the type of calendar that we hang on our walls. All that has been found are date inscriptions on tombs and monuments. For decades, no one knew what date they correlated to in the Gregorian calendar. Archeologists would find a date on a Mayan monument. But did the date refer to 1000 AD or 1000 BC, or something in between? Nobody knew.

"Until they found Stele C."

"Stella See?"

"Not Stella; Stele. A stele is a stone monument, something like a headstone, with engraving on it. The famous Rosetta stone was an Egyptian stele. The ancient peoples would carve into the stone for posterity.

"On Stele C, archeologists found carvings depicting the Maize God setting three hearthstones. It had a Mayan date at the top of the stone, *4 Ahaw 8 Cumku*, and another inscription, *thirteen baktun*, at the bottom. Thompson claimed that was the Mayan date for the beginning of the Universe.

"The only problem was, what did 4 Ahaw 8 Cumku translate to in the Christian calendar? Since there were no ancient Maya around to translate it, a correlation point had to be found, something that was dated in the Mayan world and in the Western world. The ideal thing would have been the arrival of the Spanish on the shores of Central America. But, unfortunately, Father de Landa had destroyed all the ancient Mayan manuscripts. Or, I should say, nearly all.

"Remember the Dresden Codex? It contained eclipse tables. Eclipses make ideal correlation points, because we can date them precisely. We know the date it happened in our calendar, and the Dresden Codex depicted the date it happened in the Mayan calendar. So, Thompson correlated the eclipse dates on the Dresden Codex with the inscription on Stele C. From that single monument inscription, he extrapolated an entire calendar. And he said that calendar would end in 2012.

"Since that time, many people have climbed onboard the 2012 bandwagon, trying to capitalize on the notoriety of 2012 and make pay dirt out of it. And each time the legitimate Mayan scholars poked holes in their theories they would move the goal posts.

"For instance, one popular theory claimed that in 2012, the earth would move through a photon belt. The only problem is, there is no such thing as a photon belt. Photons are packets of light energy. They do not remain stationary; light travels in all directions, so the idea that there is a belt of light that remains in the same place is ludicrous.

"Another hypothesis says that 2012 marks the end of the precession of the equinox."

"The equator?"

"The equinox. Our planet wobbles slightly on its axis as it rotates, something like a gyroscope."

"My brother had one of those when we were kids. Weird."

"As the planet spins, it points toward different stars. The North Star or Pole Star changes. It goes through its cycle ever twenty-six thousand years. The end-daters say that 2012 marks the end of the precession, and thus, the end of the world.

"The only problem is, determining the end of the precession is not like sighting the crosshairs of a rifle. There is a window, and it is about fifty years wide. So, no one can predict a precise date. Besides which, astronomers believe that our planet is about five billion years old, give or take. That means that our globe has gone through approximately a hundred ninety-two thousand, three hundred seven precessions…"

"Give or take."

"Give or take. Right. At any rate, if nothing untoward happened to the planet on those previous hundred and ninety-two thousand precessions, why should this one be any different?"

"Why, indeed?"

"And then, of course, there is the ever-popular Terence McKenna. He postulated that the ancient Maya knew that we would drop the atomic bomb on Hiroshima on August 6, 1945. He devised a complicated set of formula he called the *Timewave Generator*, saying that there are peaks and valleys in human history that can be charted along a time continuum, and that our world will end in 2012. The only problem is, after his death, a number of different mathematicians went through his equations and came up with the date 1995; not 2012. Apparently, he could postulate end-dates, but he couldn't add.

"And every time that the end-daters came up with a new theory, the Mayan scholars would prove them wrong. And Thompson became more and more defensive as time went on. He figured he had to stand his ground, and thus, he made the biggest mistake of his career. In order to verify his 2012 end-date, he published his *Commentary on the Dresden Codex*. The whole end-date argument revolved around correlating that document to the Mayan calendar, in conjunction with the inscription on

Stele C. Thompson aligned each of the eclipses in the Dresden Codex with a Mayan date determined by 2012.

"The problem was, that in order to make 2012 work, Thompson stated that the primary entry date, the base date, of the Dresden Codex was a lunar eclipse that occurred on the twelfth of November, in 755 AD. That meant that the Dresden Codex was written in the Eighth Century.

"A raging debate erupted. Enter the intrepid archeologists, Harvey and Victoria Bricker. Comparing artwork found on the codex to that found on post-classical monuments, they were convinced that the Dresden Codex came from a much later time period. Besides which, they argued that it stretched the limits of credulity to imagine that a manuscript painted on bark could have possibly survived in the hot, humid climate of the Yucatan, conditions that were notoriously harsh on manuscripts.

"That was basically where the debate stood for decades, Thompson standing his ground, refusing to budge an inch, at odds with other Mayan archeologists, but with no one being able to conclusively prove, one way or the other, the exact dating of the Mayan calendar.

"Until…"

"Oh, I love this part. Every good story always has an *until*."

He nodded, then continued. "Until Carbon 14 dating appeared in the scientific arsenal. The Brickers had the Dresden Codex dated, and the date that was arrived at was 1230 AD, plus or minus 130 years. That's the way the dating works, one gets only a ballpark figure, not a precise date; nothing like *August fourth, at three o'clock in the afternoon*. Still, it was close enough to prove, beyond the shadow of a doubt, that the Dresden Codex was created in the Thirteenth Century, and not the Eight Century, as Thompson had claimed. That, of course, shot holes in his 2012 theory.

"However, he was not to be thwarted so easily. He declared, *The uncritical acceptance of the new [Carbon 14] process savored too much of dancing round the Golden Calf for my liking.* Thompson then argued that the Dresden Codex had been damaged in the World War Two fire bombing of February 13 to 15, 1945, rendering the carbon dating inaccurate.

"When it was then determined that the codex suffered water damage, ironically, and not fire damage, not to mention that the artwork was from a later period, Thompson again countered with the claim that the Dresden Codex might have been written in the Thirteenth Century, but that it was copied from an earlier codex created in the Eighth Century, so therefore, his 2012 dating was still accurate.

"Again, check and stalemate. The problem was, no one could prove that Thompson's eclipse dates were incorrect.

"All that changed with the advent of the modern computer. Before that time, there was no accurate eclipse table for ancient Mesoamerican astronomy. The Brickers asked the royal astronomers if they could construct eclipse and planetary tables stretching back into the dim mists of prehistory, designed specifically for ancient Central America.

"The astronomers were able to deliver tables going back thousands of years. The Brickers painstakingly compared the eclipses, one by one, to the Dresden Codex, to see if they could find matches. It was a long, arduous process, but in the course of their work, they discovered something disturbing. The dates that Thompson used in his work to verify his 2012 correlation were not the same dates as enumerated on the Dresden Codex. Thompson had altered the Mayan dates!

"When the Brickers confronted him on this manipulation of data, Thompson said that he had to change the Mayan codex dates because the Dresden Codex contained what he termed *discrepancies*. At another time, he stated that the Dresden Codex had certain *irregularities* that he had to correct. He said that he used the dates that the Maya meant to write down."

"So, he was a liar. He fudged the dates."

"Exactly. He could not make the actual Mayan dates work into his 2012 theory, so he conveniently massaged the data. He committed the cardinal sin of the scientific method. He had changed the data to fit the theory instead of changing the theory to fit the data. But there is something more going on here. Think about it for a moment. What is wrong with this picture? The whole end-date argument revolves around the fact that the Maya were such astute astronomers, such meticulous mathematicians, and such scrupulous record-keepers that they could predict the end of the world thousands of years before the fact. But, if, as Thompson claims, the Mayan had errors in their eclipse tables, then that blows the end-daters right out of the water.

"As the Brickers continued to delve into the Dresden Codex dates, they discovered something even more devastating to the end-daters' argument. The dates that Thompson had chosen to prove his 2012 hypothesis did not match the computer-generated astronomical tables. Thompson used November twelfth, 755 as a base date, but there was no lunar eclipse on that date. What was more, the solar eclipses that Thompson had selected as irrefutable evidence were not even visible in the Yucatan. Ask me how could he possibly have made such an egregious mistake?"

"How could he have made such an… a mistake?"

"Funny you should ask."

She chuckled. "So, tell me."

"I will. He was using tables designed for London, England." He paused, thought, then went on. "If I told you that I was going to build a house, and you asked me, 'Do you have a hammer?' And I said, 'Nope, I don't have a hammer, but I'm going to build a house.' And then, you asked me, 'Do you have a saw?' And I said, 'Nope, I don't have a saw, but I'm going to build a house.' And you asked me, 'Do you have any nails?' and I said, 'Nope, I don't have any nails, but I'm going to build a house.' What would you say then?"

"If you don't have a hammer or a saw or nails? I'd say that you weren't going to build a house at all."

"Exactly. I couldn't build a house because I lacked the proper equipment. And the same thing goes for Thompson. He couldn't break the Mayan code because he did not have the proper tools. He was trying to use lunar tables designed for England. There was no way, no matter how hard he tried, that he would ever, not in a million years, ever determine the eclipses for the Yucatan, hence, there was just no way that he would ever arrive at the correct date for the Mayan calendar. He simply did not have the proper tools to get the job done."

"You mean, they didn't know when the eclipses would occur back then?"

"The Europeans didn't know. At least, not the eclipses that occurred in Central America. There was no reason for them to know. Remember, the Europeans did not even know that America existed before Columbus' discovery. There is a famous story of how Columbus fooled the natives into feeding his sailors. By his fourth voyage, the natives were upset with the ill-treatment that they were receiving at the hands of the conquerors. So, they refused to supply food to the Spaniards. As it happened, thanks to synchronicity, there was a lunar eclipse on February 29, 1504."

"Wait a minute. February only has twenty-eight days."

"It was a leap year. At any rate, Columbus, knowing that the eclipse would take place that night, told the natives that he would shut off the moon's light if they did not feed his sailors. The eclipse came, the natives were thrown into a panic, and they consented to feed the sailors if Columbus would turn the moon back on. He went into his hut, waited out the eclipse, and then emerged, as did the moon, much to their relief."

"I thought you just said that no one knew about American eclipses."

"That one happened to be a lunar eclipse. Lunar eclipses are visible at a location, if the moon is above the horizon at that particular location at the time of the eclipse. And on that particular occasion, it was."

"Lucky for Columbus."

"Not luck; synchronicity. I told you this story is fraught with them. Anyway, as I was saying, a solar eclipse is a different thing entirely. They are only visible on a comparatively narrow band of real estate. That's why people hop aboard planes and fly to New Zealand or South Africa, to witness a solar eclipse. In that instance, Columbus lucked out. If the eclipse had been a solar eclipse, and not visible in Central America, the outcome might have been far different, and the history of our country would have taken a decidedly different turn."

"So, Thompson was caught red-handed."

"Exactly. With his hand in the cookie jar."

"How did he weasel his way out of that one?"

"He always had an explanation for everything. In this case, he proclaimed, and I quote, *Maya astronomy is too important to be left to the astronomers.* That is a direct quote. It showed his arrogance and his total disregard for the facts."

"But once the eclipse tables were available, other Mayan scholars began doing their own research. For instance, let me show you what Vladimir and Bohumil Bohm had to say." He pulled a notebook from his case, riffled through the pages until he found what he wanted. He tapped his finger on the page as he read. "They compared the dates generated by the 2012 end-date and concluded that, *working with the Mayan data of the Dresden Codex we found out, that the Goodman-Martinez-Thompson correlation is unusable, even for the dates evidently concerning certain astronomical phenomena, as the observations of Venus visibility, or Sun and Moon eclipses. When using Thompson's Correlation for converting the dates relating to celestial phenomena into our calendar we find that the observed phenomenon would not take place.*"

"In other words, it didn't work."

"In other words, it didn't work, and they proved it. The whole end-dater argument is suspect. Remember I mentioned Stele C?"

"Uh huh." She actually did not, but she wanted to humor him. Besides, she was not prepared to sit through a recapitulation of his tale.

"The whole end-dater argument revolves around it. Basically, without the date on Stele C, they have no argument. The kicker is, what they describe as a date is not a date at all.

"Mayan monument dates are composed of a long count date followed by a calendar round date, if the inscription is horizontal, as on a monument, or if the stone is vertical, like a stele, then the long count date appears above the calendar round. And the separate dates are always adjacent to one another.

"But, on Stele C, the two are not joined, they are separated. What is more, the calendar round appears above the long count, defying their usual convention. What is more telling, the Maya always preceded their long count days with an ISIG."

"A what?"

"It stands for *initial series introductory glyph*. Every Mayan long count date is preceded by this inscription. But, it appears nowhere on Stele C. Not the least of which is, *thirteen baktun* is not written as a long count date at all, that is, thirteen followed by a series of zero glyphs. It is simply written as *thirteen baktun*.

"After much study, I came to the only possible conclusion. On Stele C, *thirteen baktun* is not meant to be a long count date at all; it is meant to be a period of time. "The phrase *thirteen baktun* appears over and over again in the Mayan texts and inscriptions, just as in the *Bible*, the term *forty* appears time and time again. I never paid much attention to the term *forty*, until I heard an Arab use the phrase, *the burden of forty camels*. He used it as we would say that we were carrying *the weight of the world upon our shoulders*. And then, I came upon it in the *Bible*, in Second Kings, chapter eight, verse nine, where it refers to *forty camels' burden* , and I suddenly realized that the term *forty* was an ancient expression that was used to mean *a great number*, just as we would say *never in a million years*. We do not mean, literally, a million years; what we mean is merely *a great deal of time.* The term was a colloquialism signifying a long period of time. It appears in the *Bible* over and over again. Here, I'll show you." He opened his briefcase and produced a *Bible.*"

"You carry a *Bible* with you?"

"Doesn't everyone?"

She rolled her eyes, but he was too busy thumbing through the pages to notice. Finally, he found what he wanted. "Here, I have them listed here." He ran his finger down the list, reading: *"It rained for forty days and forty nights (Genesis 7:12), And your children shall wander in the Wilderness forty years(Numbers 14:33) and the children of Israel ate manna for forty years (Exodus 16:35), Moses was in the midst of the cloud for forty days (Exodus 24:18), Moses But with whom was he grieved forty Years(Hebrews 3:17) and they searched the land for forty days (Numbers 13:25 Numbers 14:34), and shall ye bear your Iniquities, even forty years (Numbers 14:34) Then fled Moses at this saying, and was A stranger in the land of Madian (Acts 7:29) And when forty years were expired, there Appeared to him in the wilderness of Mount Sinai an angel of the Lord in a Flame of fire in a bush. (Acts 7:30) Forty stripes he may give him (Deuteronomy 25:3) The land had rest forty years (Judges 5:31) And the country Was in quietness forty years (Judges 8:28) And the time that Solomon reigned in Jerusalem over all Israel was forty Years (1Kings 11:42 2Chronicles 9:30) And the days that David reigned over Israel were forty years (1Kings 2:11) Jehu Jehoash Began to reign; and forty years reigned He in Jerusalem (2Kings 12:1) Joash was seven years old when he began To reign, and he reigned forty years in Jerusalem (2Chronicles 24:1) And Solomon had forty thousand stalls of Horses for his chariots (1Kings 4:26) thou Shalt bear the iniquity of the house of Judah forty days (Ezekiel 4:6) And the Lord said land of Egypt shall be desolate And waste (Ezekiel 29:9) No foot of man shall pass through it, Nor foot of beast shall pass through it, Neither shall it be inhabited forty Years (Ezekiel 29:11 Ezekiel 29:12) And when he had fasted forty days and Forty nights (Matthew 4:2) And he was there in the wilderness forty Days, tempted of Satan (Mark 1:13 Luke 4:2) Jews Banded together, and bound themselves Under a curse, saying that they would Neither eat nor drink till they had Killed Paul. And they were more than forty which had Made this conspiracy. (Acts 23:12 Acts 23:21)."*

All the time he was reciting his list, she was staring up at the ceiling, waiting for him to finish. When he paused, she asked, "You finally through?"

"I could go on."

"Please spare me. You've made your point." She thought. "What was the point you were trying to make, again?"

"Simply that *thirteen baktun* is not a date at all. It simply means *a great amount of time.* In the same sense that we would say, *for an eternity,* or, *forever and a day.* It's an expression, not an exact period of time. Just as the Biblical scribes used the term *forty,* in the ancient Biblical vernacular it signified a long period of time, the term *thirteen baktun,* to the Maya, was an extensive period of time. Like in Genesis, where it says that the world was created in six days, it doesn't literally mean that it took six days to create the Universe; it's merely a turn of phrase. Poetic license, if you will. I rest my case."

"Good. Please, do me a favor; by all means, rest your case." She snapped her gum decisively.

He cleared his throat. "The whole end-dater argument hinges on 4 Ahaw 8 Cumku being the beginning of the Mayan calendar.

"But, 4 Ahaw 8 Cumku cannot possibly be the first day of the Mayan calendar. What is the first day of the Gregorian calendar? Day 1, Month 1, Year 1. In other words, the first day of the Christian calendar is the first day of the first month of the first year. But consider the Mayan date: 4 Ahaw 8 Cumku. That is like saying the fourth day of the eighth month.

What happened to the third day? Or the second day? Or the seventh month, or the sixth month, or the fifth month, and so on, down the line?

"In the Tzolkin calendar, the day and the number were both incremented by one. In our system, it would be equivalent to numbering the days, *1 Sunday, 2 Monday, 3 Tuesday, 4 Wednesday*, et cetera. The Haab consisted of the month and the day number; in our calendar it would be *1 January, 2 January, 3 January*, et cetera, all the way to *31 January, 1 February, 2 February, 3 February, 4 February*, et cetera.

"The first day of the Mayan calendar, therefore, would not be *4 Ahaw 8 Cumku*, but more rightly *1 Ahaw 0 Cumku*. If the Maya were meticulous mathematicians, they would have logically commenced their calendar on the first day of the first month, not the fourth day of the eighth month. By a careful examination of the Mayan calendar round, it is obvious that whatever *4 Ahaw 8 Cumku* designates, it is definitely *not* the beginning of their calendar. Just as the Gregorian calendar commences on the first day of the first month of the first year, the Mayan calendar likewise would have started on the first day of the first month, not on the fourth day of the eighth month.

"Let us look at this logically. Our calendar is based on the birth of Christ, but it starts on January 1, not on December 25. Now, if you saw this…" he wrote on the pad:

Day Month Year
1   1   1

"…you would automatically think, the first day of the first month of the first year. Now, if you saw this…"

Day Month Year
25   12   1

"…you would think, the twenty-fifth day of the twelfth month. In this case, you would discern that it was preceded by the twenty-fourth day of the twelfth month, and the twenty-third day of the twelfth month, et cetera, and then by all the days of the eleventh month, and all the days of the tenth month, et cetera. So, if you saw…"

Day   Month   Year
4   8   1

"…you would deduce that it was preceded by the seventh month, and the sixth month, et cetera. By extension then, when we observe a Mayan calendar round date of 4 Ahaw 8 Cumku, we can logically assume that it cannot possibly be the start of the Mayan calendar. And if 4 Ahaw 8 Cumku is not the beginning of the Mayan calendar, then 2012 cannot possibly be the end of the Mayan calendar.

"The actual fact of the matter is, we do not know what date 4 Ahaw 8 Cumku represents, and unfortunately, there are no ancient Maya who have survived to tell us, but if the Maya were as logical and methodical and meticulous as the end-daters would have us believe, then they would have initiated their calendar on the first day of the first month and not the fourth day of the eighth month. On the one hand, we are led to believe that the Maya were so methodical that they could predict the future unerringly. But on the other hand, we are told that they were not logical enough to begin their calendar on the first day of the first month. What is wrong with this picture?" He spread his hands wide and clapped them together with a resounding boom.

"The average person on the street just naturally believes that there is only one end-date. The fact of the matter is, not even the end-daters can decide on the exact date. Even Goodman couldn't make up his mind. Originally, he said that it was December 18. Then, later on, he changed it to December 21.

"Even the so-called self-proclaimed experts can't come to an agreement on that account. Thompson initially said December 23, then switched it to December 21. Martinez claimed December 19. Floyd Lounsbury claimed December 24, while David Freidel said it is December 23, and Beyer said December 22. Suchtelen said that it is December 23, but not December 23, 2012, December 23, 2011. Carl

2012

Johan Calleman said that they were all wrong, because they forgot to factor in leap years or the not insignificant fact that the Gregorian calendar has no zero year. He said it is 2011, but October 28, 2011. And Jose Antonio Villacorta Calderon, referring to Dresden Almanacs 40 and 47, and what he considers to be irrefutable evidence, cites a day, not 2011 or 2012, but in the year 2013 and not December 21, but January 21.

"So, even among the aficionados of the 2012 end-date we find considerable disagreement. The end-date is either 2011 or 2012 or 2013. And the day is either December 18 or 19 or 21 or 22 or 23 or 24 or October 28 or January 21. Take your pick.

"But, that's just the start of it. Take a look at this." He fished around in his case and came up with a sheaf of papers. Look at these. These are different Mayan calendar dates postulated by different Mayan scholars."

He showed her the following table:

1)	Robert Heneling	-1,382,316	1 Apr 8498 BC	10 Aug 3373 BC
2)	Charles Bowditch	394,483	16 Dec 3634 BC	26 Apr 1493 AD
3)	Willson	438,906	31 Jul 3512 BC	11 Dec 1614 AD
4)	Bunge	449,817	16 June 3482 BC	25 Oct 1644 AD
5)	Charles H. Smiley	482,699	26 June 3392 BC	5 Nov 1734 AD
6)	Smiley	482,914	27 Jan 3391 BC	8 June 1735 AD
7)	Nancy K. Owen	487,410	20 May 3379 BC	29 Sep 1747 AD
8)	M. Makemson	489,138	11 Feb 3374 BC	22 June 1752 AD
9)	Spinden	489,383	14 Oct 3374 BC	22 Feb 1753 AD
10)	Herbert Spinden	489,384	15 Oct 3374 BC	23 Feb 1753 AD
11)	Ludendorff	489,484	23 Jan 3373 BC	3 June 1753 AD
12)	Teeple	492,622	26 Aug 3365 BC	5 Jan 1762 AD
13)	Dinsmoor	497,878	16 Jan 3350 BC	27 May 1776 AD
14)	Smiley	500,210	5 Jun 3344 BC	15 Oct 1782 AD
15)	Hochleitner	507,994	27 Sept 3323 BC	7 Feb 1804 AD
16)	Hochleitner	508,362	30 Sept 3322 BC	9 Feb 1805 AD
17)	Hochleitner	525,698	19 Mar 3274 BC	28 Jul 1852 AD
18)	D. H. Kelley	550,279	6 Jul 3207 BC	16 Nov 1919 AD
19)	Kelley	553,279	22 Sept 3199 BC	2 Feb 1928 AD

2012

20)	Martin	563,334	3 Apr 3171 BC	14 Aug 1955 AD
21)	Hochleitner	577,264	23 May 3133 BC	3 Oct 1993 AD
22)	Hochleitner	578,585	4 Jan 3129 BC	16 May 1997 AD
23)	Carl Calleman	583,863	17 June 3115 BC	28 Oct 2011 AD
24)	Suchtelen	583,919	12 Aug 3115 BC	23 Dec 2011 AD
25)	Goodman (1905)	584,280	8 Aug 3114 BC	18 Dec 2012 AD
26)	Martínez	584,281	9 Aug 3114 BC	19 Dec 2012 AD
27)	J. T. Goodman	584,283	11 Aug 3114 BC	21 Dec 2012 AD
28)	Martínez	584,283	11 Aug 3114 BC	21 Dec 2012 AD
29)	Thompson (1950)	584,283	11 Aug 3114 BC	21 Dec 2012 AD
30)	Nowotny	584,283	11 Aug 3114 BC	21 Dec 2012 AD
31)	Beyer	584,284	12 Aug 3114 BC	22 Dec 2012 AD
32)	Grube	584,285	13 Aug 3114 BC	23 Dec 2012 AD
33)	Sabloff	584,285	13 Aug 3114 BC	23 Dec 2012 AD
34)	David Freidel	584,285	13 Aug 3114 BC	23 Dec 2012 AD
35)	Malmström	584,285	13 Aug 3114 BC	23 Dec 2012 AD
36)	Linda Schele	584,285	13 Aug 3114 BC	23 Dec 2012 AD
37)	Thompson (1935)	584,285	13 Aug 3114 BC	23 Dec 2012 AD
38)	Floyd Lounsbury	584,285	13 Aug 3114 BC	23 Dec 2012 AD
39)	Lounsbury	584,286	14 Aug 3114 BC	24 Dec 2012 AD
40)	Calderon	584,314	11 Sept 3114 BC	21 Jan 2013 AD
41)	Cook	585,789	25 Sept 3110 BC	4 Feb 2017 AD
42)	Mukerji	588,466	23 Jan 3102 BC	4 Jun 2024 AD
43)	Alexander Pogo	588,626	2 Jul 3102 BC	11 Nov 2024 AD
44)	Schove	594,250	25 Nov 3087 BC	5 Apr 2040 AD
45)	Hochleitner	609,417	4 Jun 3045 BC	4 Oct 2081 AD
46)	Schove	615,824	19 Dec 3028 BC	30 Apr 2099 AD
47)	Bohm	622,261	4 Aug 3010 BC	14 Dec 2116 AD
48)	Kaucher	626,660	21 Aug 2998 BC	30 Dec 2128 AD
49)	Kreichgauer	626,927	14 May 2997 BC	23 Sep 2129 AD
50)	Hochleitner	660,205	24 Jun 2906 BC	30 Dec 2128 AD
51)	Wells/Fuls	660,208	27 Jun 2906 BC	6 Nov 2220 AD
52)	Kelley	663,310	25 Dec 2898 BC	5 May 2229 AD
53)	Hochleitner	674,265	22 Dec 2868 BC	3 May 2259 AD
54)	Hochleitner	674,927	15 Oct 2866 BC	23 Feb 2261 AD
55)	Schulz	677,723	11 Jun 2858 BC	20 Oct 2268 AD
56)	Escalona Ramos	679,100	19 Mar 2854 BC	28 Jul 2272 AD
57)	Escalona	679,108	27 Mar 2854 BC	23 Feb 2261 AD
58)	Vaillant	679,183	10 Jun 2854 BC	19 Oct 2272 AD
59)	Wauchope	679,183	10 Jun 2854 BC	19 Oct 2272 AD

60)	Dittrich	698,163	28 May 2802 BC	7 Oct 2324 AD
61)	Verbelen	739,601	9 Nov 2689 BC	21 Mar 2438 AD
62)	R. B. Weitzel	774,078	3 Apr 2594 BC	12 Aug 2532 AD
63)	A. L. Vollemaere	774,080	5 Apr 2594 BC	14 Aug 2532 AD
64)	Vaillant	774,083	8 Apr 2594 BC	17 Aug 2532 AD
65)	Linda Schele	(20 Baktun)	13 Aug 3114 BC	13 Oct 4772 AD
66)	Palenque Stele	1,973,280	22 Jul 690 AD	2 Dec 5815 AD

"What are these funny numbers?" she asked.

"Those are Julian day numbers. You see, in our calendar, we have AD and BC, or in the modern terminology, C.E. for *Common Era* and B.C.E., meaning *Before the Common Era*. That way, non-Christians won't be offended."

"Political correctness."

"Right. Since our calendar has no zero year, that is, the first year is the year one AD, and the year before that is the year one BC. But, there is no *year zero*. It makes it all very confusing when one is determining long time spans, especially for things like comets, so astronomers devised the *Julian date*. They started with the year one and just increment from there. In that way, every date in history has a positive number. If makes calculations much simpler. I've been saying 2012, but technically, the Thompson correlation, or *GMT*, is 584283. But 2012 is a whole lot easier than saying 584283, and when I shorten it to 283, no one knows what I'm talking about. So, just for the sake of the discussion, I shortened it to 2012.

"Thanks; I appreciate that. When you scientists try to make things easier, all you do is make them harder." She studied the chart. "Those are all Mayan calendar end-dates?"

"That's right. Every scholar has their own theory. What does that tell you?"

"That, obviously, they're not cut in stone."

He laughed. "You're right about that. Just look at the range. They date all the way from 3373 BC to 5815 AD. Now, applying Common Sense Logic, if the dates differed by a few days or even a few weeks or a few months, one might attribute it to a simple error in computation. But when you see dates differing by over nine thousand years, that can only mean one thing - there is a gigantic hole in their logic."

"So, which one is the right one?"

"That, my dear, is the sixty-four thousand dollar question."

"Do you happen to have a sixty-four thousand dollar answer?"

"I do. And it's not up my sleeve. Now that the microprocessor was available, several Mayan scholars decided to put it to work solving the Mayan calendar issue, once and for all. For instance, R. B. Weitzel, and A. L. Vollemaere came up with the idea of working the Dresden Codex backwards, plugging every date on the Dresden Codex into the computer and seeing if they would all correlate to a single common date.

"They crunched the numbers and the Julian date they arrived at was 774080, yielding an end-date of 2532. If one inputs Thompson's 2012 into the Dresden Codex, it matches about fifty percent of the lunar eclipses, which is understandable, since lunar eclipses are visible on a fairly large section of the planet. But the solar eclipses are a different matter entirely. In that case, 2012 yields zero matches. As far as the transits of Venus are concerned, zero. And the transits of Mars, same thing, a big fat goose egg.

"But, when the end-date of 2532 is input into the codex, it matches one hundred percent of the lunar eclipses. Solar eclipses, one hundred percent. Transit of Venus, one hundred percent. Transit of Mars, one hundred percent."

"So, they hit the nail right on the head. They found the right date."

"Correct. But, as it turns out, an archeologist by the name of George C. Vaillant, had already determined that way back in the nineteen thirties. At the time, no one would listen to him, his voice was completely drowned out by Thompson's."

"The squeaky wheel gets the grease."

"You got that right. His is an interesting case, though. Way back when, when all the other Mayan archeologists were trying to correlate the Mayan calendar with the Gregorian calendar, Vaillant told them that they were using the wrong approach."

"Not using Common Sense Logic?"

"Right. Whereas all the others were principally Mayan archeologists, Vaillant was an Aztec archeologist. His contention was that both the Mayan calendar and the Aztec calendar were based on the Olmec calendar, an earlier race in Mesoamerica. Therefore, Vaillant argued, since the Aztec calendar was already dated, it made more sense to correlate the Mayan calendar with the Aztec calendar than with the Gregorian calendar, with which it had absolutely nothing in common.

"He was right all along, and if anyone had bothered to listen to him, we all would have been light-years ahead. He was finally vindicated, but it took the better part of a century, and unfortunately, not until after his death."

"So, he died without ever knowing he was right?"

"Oh, I think he knew that he was right. He pointed out a number of inconsistencies in applying the 2012 end-date to the Mayan calendar, such as, if one used that date, then one was left with the absurd contradiction that the Aztec conquered the Mayan centuries before the Aztec even entered Mexico from the north, a logical impossibility. But Vaillant pointed out something that had escaped the notice of the other Mayanists. If one accepted Thompson's dating of the Mayan calendar, and applied it to their structures, then that would leave a gap of some five hundred years in the Mayan timeline when no Mayan monuments were erected and no inscriptions whatsoever were made. It was as if their civilization had simply vanished for five centuries, and then magically reappeared. In effect, it left a huge gaping hole in the history of the Maya.

"At any rate, the upshot is, using vastly different approaches, they had all proved the same thing, coming from different directions. Thompson's 2012 end-date was wrong. He had managed to fool people, because on the surface, that round count quirk in the Mayan calendar can be very confusing. Because it continues to cycle every 52 years, it can appear to be the correct date even when it is not. Just because the haab day matches doesn't mean that the long count date matches. Just like in our calendar, July Fourth can fall on a Monday in 1966, 1977, 1983, or 1994. Knowing the month and the day tells one absolutely nothing about the year.

"But, look carefully at the numbers." She leaned over to get a better view.

"You see, the calendar round cycles every 52 years." He wrote down a large 52. "Now watch this. Take Thompson's 2012 and subtract it from their 2532." He wrote the numbers down, one above the other.

"Five hundred thirty-two," she said.

He nodded, writing down the correct figure. "Exactly. Five hundred twenty." He tapped his pen on the yellow pad. "Do you see the factor between the two?" He added a zero behind the 52 to make 520. "Five hundred twenty is ten times fifty-two. They had the right day and month, but they were exactly ten calendar rounds off the mark."

He set the pen down. "Have you ever heard of Atlantis?"

"Sure. Everyone has."

"Well, in deciphering the story of Atlantis, some scholars say that Plato was referring to a time that was nine thousand years ago, and others say that he meant ninety thousand. The difference of a single letter in an ancient script can make a mighty big difference in the actual number. Take the difference between a million and a billion, for instance. One tiny letter, but what a big difference that single letter makes. Even more so between cultures. Our billion is a one followed by nine zeros, but to the

British, a billion is a one followed by twelve zeroes. So, their billion is our trillion.

"Applying the same logic to the Mayan calendar, Goodman and Thompson were ten calendar rounds off. In a manner of speaking, one might say that they had their decimal point in the wrong place. But, even beyond that, there is another huge problem with their 2012 date. Thompson claimed that the Mayan calendar would end when the creation date recycled. The creation date found on Stele C is 4 Ahaw 8 Cumku. So, the Mayan calendar, according to them, would end when it recycled to 4 Ahaw 8 Cumku. The problem is, 2012 is not 4 Ahaw 8 Cumku; it's 4 Ahaw 3 Kankin. They violated their own parameters. Using their own criteria, there is no way that it recycles, or ends, on 2012. They did not prove themselves right; they proved themselves wrong."

"So then, the correct date is 2532; not 2012."

"There are still some huge problems, even with that date. The earliest it could possibly be is 2532. That is, if the Mayan calendar actually cycles on the thirteenth baktun.

"However, there is no valid reason to believe that it does. The Maya used the vigesimal numbering system, with a base of twenty. The other wheels on their long count calendar cycle at twenty, not thirteen. The archeologist, Linda Schele, has found inscriptions at Palenque, referring to the ruler, Lord Pakal, which refer to his return on a twenty-baktun time frame, or a pictun. That would push the end-date all the way to October 13, 4772. And then, we have another inscription on a stele found at Palenque that would advance the end-date all the way to 5815 AD.

"But even if we disregard all of those dates and go back to their original premise, that the Mayan calendar ends when it cycles again to thirteen baktun 4 Ahaw 8 Cumku. Using their very own criteria, and doing the computation correctly, one arrives at the date of 371,039 AD."

"Wow, that's a long time to come."

"So long, in fact, that not either you or your next one hundred incarnations have to worry about it coming anytime soon."

2012

"So, what difference does it make?"

"Because of the way that we form our reality. Reality is not a solid, tangible form. It is an illusion. An illusion that we create with our thoughts, attitudes, and emotions. And if our thoughts are negative, full of doom and gloom scenarios, we create a huge bubble of negative energy that will manifest itself in negative ramifications. Billions of people, anxious about 2012 and the end of the world, will create negative manifestations. It might not be the end of the world, but for many, it might just as well be. The negative energy might create a pole shift, but it could very well manifest itself in other major earth cataclysms, such as tornadoes, hurricanes, mud slides, land slides, tidal waves, or any of a myriad other things the flesh is heir to.

"The end of the world has been predicted numerous times down through the ages. The most famous, of course, occurred in 999 AD. Believing the purveyors of doom and gloom, the medieval peasants neglected to plant their crops, in anticipation of the end of the world, due to arrive promptly when the calendar turned 1000. Imagine their surprise then, after killing off their livestock, and carrying on for days on end, carousing, rabble-rousing, pillaging, and plundering, and in general, eating, drinking, and being merry, when they awoke on the morning of 1000 AD, only to find the world perfectly intact, and themselves none the worse for wear, except for the aftereffects of their merriment. The only problem was, there were no crops to be harvested, no farm animals left to be butchered. The result was mass starvation. So, in a tragic twist of fate, the end-of-the-world prophesy did come true for many people that year.

"Another terrible disaster occurred in 1666. As that year approached, people were certain that the combination of the one thousand and the 666, or the sign of the beast, foretold the end of the world. Once again, their negative emotions did create the end for many, in the form of a bubonic plague and the Great Fire of London that claimed over a hundred thousand souls. Was it the end of the world? Well, for many, it was indeed, but only because it became a self-fulfilling prophesy.

"Edgar Cayce, the renowned psychic healer, widely known as *The Sleeping Prophet*, often stated that *mind is the builder*. What he meant by that was that we create our world, our experience, our reality. Our thoughts form our experience.

"Does that sound like a crazy idea? Well, he has the support of three thousand years of Buddhism, Hinduism, Taoism, along with Western philosophers such as Plato, Pythagoras, and even Jesus of Nazareth. And now, even the scientific community is jumping on the bandwagon. Propelled by the theories of relativity, postulated by Albert Einstein, and furthered by Heisenberg, quantum physics is propounding exactly what the sages, philosophers, seers, gurus, Zen masters, and Eastern religions have been saying for ages. The world is basically thought-form. Call it a dream, an illusion, a mental hologram, they all agree that we form, individually and en masse, our reality, our dimension, the entire Universe, for that matter. We draw energy from the Collective Unconscious and form it into our physical experience. Our reality mirrors our thoughts. If we concentrate on negativity, such as fears of the end times, our thoughts become manifest in our physical experience. If we concentrate on disaster, then we will be met with disaster. If we concentrate on fearful cataclysms, then that is what we will get.

"The bottom line? Portending the end of the world is not only nonsense, it is dangerous nonsense. Believing that disaster will befall us, fearing that disaster will occur, will create waves of negativity that will produce the desired or undesired results. We create what we fear. We bring these occurrences into our experience. Franklin Delano Roosevelt was not so far off the mark when he stated, *the only thing we have to fear is fear itself.*

"This is exactly what manifested itself in the Y2K debacle. Fear and paranoia reigned supreme. People hoarded food, built underground bunkers, and prepared for the worst. The end of computers. The end of the economy. The end of the world. Fear built upon fear, a snowball becoming an avalanche.

"The end result? The Stock Market plummeted, the economy faltered. Greed and avarice reared their ugly heads. The dot-com companies, which were nothing but phony pyramid schemes in new wineskins, began to crumble. Corporations came crashing down like a house of cards, while CEO's drifted to financial security on golden parachutes. Pension funds were raped, pillaged, and plundered; unemployment lines lengthened. People began to fear for their jobs, for their livelihoods, for their retirements. More fear, bubbling like a caldron, until it all boiled over.

2012

"Then came the terrorist attacks. New worries, new fears. More lay-offs. More company closures. More bankruptcies. The airline industry took a nose-dive, the financial system crashed and burned. More frequent terrorist alerts. Anthrax scares. More fear, more panic, more negative thoughts, manifesting themselves in more tragedy, more negative effects. A vicious circle had begun, like a snake eating its own tail. Roosevelt was right. All we had to fear was fear itself. The negativity of our collective thoughts, our collective fears, had exploded in a torrent of human misery. Our worst fears were becoming reality. To coin a phrase, *if we think it, it will come.*

"Proclaiming the end of the world in 2012 will have the effect of causing a great deal of panic and worry. Some people are already planning for the disaster. Years of anxiety and negative thinking, amassed by countless numbers of people expecting and fearing the worst, will only result in horrendous negative ramifications. The after-effects of Y2K will be small potatoes in comparison to the adverse effects of the negative thinking prompted by 2012 panic."

"So, what can we do about it?"

"We can do what we were meant to do. Each one of us is here for a reason, a purpose. We're on a mission."

"Really?" she asked, wide-eyed. "Every one of us? Even me?"

"Every one of us," he replied. "Even you."

She considered for a moment, deep in thought. "How am I supposed to know what my mission is?"

"It's all about synchronicities. Let me tell you a little story."

She pulled her knees toward her chest and wrapped her arms around her legs, snuggling up.

He began. "Bright and early one Saturday morning, a long long time ago, I set out with a list of errands to run. As I pulled to a stop at a traffic light, I could not help noticing the vehicle in front of me - an ancient dilapidated rusted Volkswagen bus. The only thing holding it together was some cracked bonding putty and the vast array of bumper stickers plastered across its entire tail end. Sporting slogans, mottoes, catch phrases, accumulated over the span of several decades, the vehicle was a regular museum of modern art on wheels.

"I began reading, chuckling to myself as I revisited the anthems of my youth: *Make love, not war. It takes both the sun and rain to make a rainbow. If you love something, set it free. Today's the first day of the rest of your life. Give peace a chance.*

"I was about halfway through the array of stickers when the traffic light turned green, and for the first time in my life, I wanted the light to stay red longer. As the van pulled away from me, I depressed the accelerator, trying to keep up with it, so that I could finish my reading, but the van had a surprisingly lot of spunk for a vehicle of its vintage. It sped off, changed lanes, then exited on the next ramp, and that was the last I saw of it. Or so I thought. Stay tuned.

"I proceeded on my way. First stop: the mall. As I was getting out of the car, a dog barked loudly. Startled, I jumped at the sound. I looked into the car, expecting to be devoured by a huge hungry mongrel, no doubt foaming at the mouth, a rabid pit bull.

"Much to my surprise, the huge bark was coming from a tiny little dog, barely bigger than a rat. A new breed of rat-dog. No hair, no fur whatsoever. With a maw as big as its entire head. Wearing a diamond-studded collar that would have made the crown jewels envious, it was standing on the back of the seat, barking up a storm. The window was cracked a bit for ventilation, and I suppose that the sound, reverberating around the car's interior, was somehow magnified like a loudspeaker. I had been in mortal fear for my life, over a dog that I could have held in one hand.

"I laughed, breathed a sigh of relief, and went into the mall to do my shopping, pushing the entire incident from my mind.

"Until later, when I came out of the mall. As I was walking down the line of cars, the episode bounced back into my head, and I wondered vaguely if the nuisance dog would still be there. Much to my relief, the dog, and the car he had been in, were nowhere in sight.

"I proceeded to run other errands, did some more shopping, and even took in a movie. Hours later, I was more than ready to call it a day.

"As I was returning home, the thought popped into my mind that I needed some milk. I was dog-tired, and the last thing I wanted to do was stop for milk. There was a large grocery store on my route, not far from my house. I could pull in there. I put on my turn signal to pull off into the parking lot, but then thought better of it. I was exhausted. The milk could wait until the next day.

"I turned the corner, and proceeded down the street. Something was nagging at my brain to get the milk. There was another entrance to the store's parking lot, along the street I was driving. I wanted to go home badly, but the nagging thought kept pressing on my brain. At the last possible moment, I changed my mind and swung into the parking lot.

"I pulled my car into the line of parked cars, opened the door and got out. Suddenly, I heard a loud barking. I froze in horror. By the sound of the dog, I was about to be torn to shreds. I jumped back.

"Then, I laughed out loud. There, in the car next to me, was a tiny little dog, barking up a storm. A dog no bigger than a mouse, making a sound like a roaring lion. At least, that was how it sounded to my ears.

"Then, something dawned on me as I recognized the dog from before. Same dog, same diamond-encrusted collar. Same spiked hairdo. Same car.

"What a coincidence, I thought. There I was, parked next to the very same car that I had parked next to earlier in the day. Hours apart, miles apart, and yet, I had somehow managed to park next to the same vehicle. What were the chances of that happening? But what was even more peculiar was that, if I had driven into the other parking lot entrance, I would have parked on the opposite end of the lot, far away from that car, and would never have even known that it was in the parking lot. The permutations and intricacies of those two events taking place was mind-boggling.

"The complexities of that bizarre coincidence were still running through my mind as I headed home. I was deep in thought when I stopped at a red light at the last set of lights on my route. I was so preoccupied that, for a moment, it did not even occur to me that I was stopped behind a van. A van covered with bumper stickers!

"My eyes almost dropped out of my head when I realized that I was behind that very same van that I had been behind that morning, so many hours before. There it was in all its glory, same rusting hulk, same cracked bonding putty, same array of stickers plastered over every available square inch of available space. I had started my day off and ended it, at the same set of traffic lights, behind the very same van. It had to be the same van; what were the chances of two such identical vans existing in the same Universe?

"But how could such a coincidence have happened? It boggled the mind. If I had left my house a minute earlier or later, I would not have been at the traffic light behind the van. If I had not stopped for milk, if I had stayed in any store a few minutes longer, or shorter. If I had not been startled by the barking dog, my travel would have been changed just enough to not have been at that same traffic light, at the end of the day, to miss that van. The intricacies were way beyond comprehension. Even if I had had the biggest, fastest, most powerful super-quantum-computer in the world, I still could not have figured out all of the permutations of those disparate events to account for every action, every decision I had made during the course of that day, to make such a complicated chain of events coincide.

"That bizarre series of events stayed with me for days afterward, haunting my thoughts. How could I put it all together?

"At the time those events occurred, I was not even aware of the expression *synchronicity*. That was a term, I was later to learn, that had been coined by the famous Swiss psychiatrist, Carl Jung, the founder of analytical psychology. Simply stated, a *synchronicity* is the coincidence of meaningfully-related events that seems to be outside the realm of cause-and-effect relationship. In other words, a *synchronicity* is a coincidence that is too coincidental to be a coincidence. For example, you are thinking of someone, the telephone rings, and guess who is on the other end of the line?"

"Or, you are speaking of the devil, and voilà, they appear," she said.

"Exactly. All I knew was that those were bizarre coincidences that were beyond the realm of mere chance. We are instilled with a strict mechanistic view of reality. Things happen for a reason. A chain of events. Connect the dots. Anything outside of that narrow scope is viewed with deep suspicion, or simply disregarded altogether. I had been firmly indoctrinated in the strict party line of the planet. One thing causes another. You start at Point A and proceed to Point B. You cannot be in two places at the same time.

"So, having experienced a number of events that had no logical rhyme or reason, I began to have grave doubts and grave questions about whether or not all that we had taken for granted was really so cut-and-dried.

"If this had been the first time such coincidences had happened, I might have been able to dismiss them. When I thought back on it, I could recall numerous other occasions when similarly bizarre situations had occurred in my life. But those specific events seemed more than the usual unusual. They seemed to be some sort of a wake-up call, so intrusive that they could not be ignored.

"I decided to start a log of all such occurrences. I called it *My Journal of Coincidences*. My intention was to record the coincidences to see if they had any common thread.

"First off, the sheer number amazed me. Looking back over my life, I was able to recall literally countless numbers of times when strange coincidences occurred to me. Not once or twice, or even a few times, but many many times.

"My notebook began to fill. What I thought would be a short exercise began to take on mammoth proportions. It was obvious that these coincidences were occurring all the time, and even more than that, that they had been occurring all of my life."

"So, why hadn't you noticed them before?"

"Good question. The more I became aware of them, the more they seemed to pop up. Was I causing them to happen because I was looking for them, or was I just becoming more aware of them? Which came first, the chicken or the egg?"

"The omelet."

He grinned. "It soon became apparent that the reason behind *the van and dog synchronicities*, for that is what I began calling them, had happened in order to awaken me to their existence. In effect, the Universe was crying out to me, no, screaming out to me, saying *notice me. See these things all around you.* I had completely overlooked them. They were there all the time, only I had completely overlooked the obvious.

"And, they were not just happening to me. Carl Jung had discovered that. He had his patients record their dreams, and in the course of events, they began relating to him strange coincidences. He soon realized that the occurrences were beyond natural laws of the Universe, and so he coined his phrase *synchronicity*.

"As my notebook, and then notebooks, began to fill up, I soon began to see that synchronicities were not the exception, but the rule. They are how reality is created. Not by cause and effect, but by synchronistic causality. They indicate the way the Universe operates, the way in which reality, and our experience is formed.

"Things started falling into place. The ancient Buddhists and Hindus and Taoists had been right all along. The world is not what it appears. The world is what we make it. Literally. And now, psychoanalysis was catching up with religion. And science, in the form of Einstein's theory of relativity and quantum physics, was following suit. In their own ways, they were all agreeing. The world was not what it seemed. And synchronicities were the clue to it all.

"Synchronicities could not possibly exist in a world governed by strict cause-and-effect relationships, any more than they could exist in a world formed by random chance. There was more to reality than meets the eye. All of our common sense assumptions about the world were in error. And the key to understanding the underpinnings of reality, the reality of reality, were locked up in synchronicities. It is how the Universe operates. What is more, since we create them, unconsciously, they indicate our modus operandi, as it were.

"As I studied my Synchronicity Journal, I began to see patterns emerging. Our lives tend to be cyclical. We go through similar occurrences, over and over again. It is obvious that we are on a learning curve. If we do not learn the lesson the first time around, then the Universe presents it to us again. And again. And again. Until we get it right."

"Like the movie, *Groundhog Day*, in which Bill Murray has to repeat the same day over and over again until he learns how *not* to be a jerk."

"Right. I saw similar patterns in my own experience. It became apparent that I, too, was repeating certain life lessons. And each time similar lessons cropped up, so would certain individuals. As I was going through the same events, the same people would appear. I would bump into childhood friends and acquaintances I had not seen in years. And unfortunately, repeat the same mistakes. Patterns. Indications. Lessons.

"Let me give you a basic example of how synchronicities work. I once lived alongside an old dirt road, always fighting the dust in the summer, the mud in the winter, and the potholes the rest of the time. Just as I was moving away, the road was finally paved.

"The amazing thing was that a similar thing happened, not once, not twice, but many times. Just about the time I was relocating, the road, the street, the highway, whatever, that I used, was repaved, repaired, fixed up.

"Now, I have come to realize that, for me, the roads represent travel, moving on to new horizons, taking me away from the tired old ways. Out with the old, in with the new. Everything that roads symbolize. And it had been happening to me all my life. Only, I had not seen the forest for the trees. Sometimes, we do not notice what is right under our noses.

"The key to spotting them is to write them down; start a synchronicity journal. Keep track of the circumstances surrounding each occurrence. This is just as important as the synchronicity itself, for it will tell you a great deal about its meaning and its relevance in your life. The pattern is a reminder. It is an alert, a red flag, a signal from the Universe.

"The entries do not have to be long or detailed. It does not have to become tedious drudgery. In my own case, I started my synchronicity journal in order to convince myself that they were, in fact, happening, and that they were not just a figment of my overactive imagination. As I collected more and more of them, their existence became undeniable. The individual entries became shorter. Eventually, just a note or two was sufficient.

"Some people say that they are not aware of any synchronicities in their lives. By the same token, some people claim that they do not dream. But, scientists who study sleep rhythms have determined that we all dream. Sleep is full of dreams; life is full of synchronicities.

"Begin with your latest *coincidence*. Write down all the circumstances surrounding it. That memory will trigger others, and soon, the associations will come flooding forth. Before long, you will begin to see that they are too coincidental to be coincidental, and furthermore, you will begin to detect patterns forming, joined by a common thread, a common denominator that is the connecting link between them all. That is the nudge that the Universe is giving you to guide you along your path.

"There is another reason for starting a Synchronicity Journal. Just by logging them, by becoming aware of them, you will begin to see more and more of them cropping up. Your antennae will go up, your synchronicity radar will switch into overdrive, and they will begin to pop out at you. It is similar to when you are in the market for a new car. Suddenly, every other car on the highway is of an identical color.

"Before buying my last car, I was not even aware that that particular model existed. But, as soon as I drove it off the car lot, it seemed as though the road were full of them. The very first time I pulled into a gas station, I got out of my car, and there, at the pump across from me, was an identical car, right down to the paint job.

"Not long after that, coming out of a shopping mall, I inserted the key into my new car, only to discover that it would not turn. Perplexed at first, I thought I was using the wrong key. I checked it to be sure, reinserted it into the lock. Still nothing. It refused to budge. It was only at that point that I happened to glance into the back seat and saw several items that did not belong to me. It suddenly dawned on me that I was trying to enter someone else's automobile. I moved away from the car, hoping that its owner had not seen me and thought that I was trying to break into their car.

"But, where was my mine? I was certain that that was exactly where I had parked. I scanned the sea of cars, and spotted mine, the very next one down the line. Another car had parked next to mine while I was in the mall. Same make, same model, same color.

"If you are beginning to hear the opening strains of *The Twilight Zone* theme song right about now, that is because another one of those profound synchronicities had occurred. They are around us all the time, but we never see them until we open our eyes to them. As the *Bible* says, *the LORD hath not given you an heart to perceive, and eyes to see, and ears to hear, unto this day.* That's in Deuteronomy, 29:4. We perceive them when we are ready for them, and if you are seeing synchronicities all around you, then that is a clear indication that you are ready to fulfill your destiny."

"So, I write them down. Then what?"

"Recording the synchronicities is only the first step. The next step is interpreting them.

"Synchronicities are specific to the person, just as dreams are individual to the dreamer. There are, of course, broad generalizations that can be made, but for the most part, they apply solely to the dreamer alone. If a national flag were held up in front of a group of people, each one of them would have their own individualized reaction to it. The emotional symbolism might be common among the group in a general sort of way, but each separate person would have their own personal response.

"We are all snowflakes, no two alike. If we were all the same, then the Universe would have no reason to make so many of us. We are each unique, links on an endless chain of humanity, no one link any more or less important than any of the others. If the chain breaks, we do not say that a link is broken; we say that the chain is broken.

"Everyone is important. The Universe is too intelligent, too wise, too omniscient, to create anything or anyone that is not valuable to the overall plan. Everyone has a purpose in life, a reason for existing.

"Open a pocket watch. You will find numerous tiny gears, each moving in perfect synchrony with the others. Remove just one of those parts and the watch stops.

"Consider your automobile engine. It has a myriad of parts. If you take one of them away, the engine ceases to run, or if it does, it does not function at as high a degree of efficiency.

"Each person is essential to the functioning of the whole. If they were not, they would not be here. The Universe, in its infinite wisdom, does not waste energy. It does not create a single being without a purpose. The point is to discover one's purpose."

"How do we do that?"

"By discerning our connection with the Universe. That connection is indicated by our synchronicities. They show how our experiences are created, and why. Let me show you an example to illustrate how the Universe operates.

"One day, as I was driving through town, I came to a four-way stop. Being an upstanding pillar of my community, and observing all of the traffic laws and regulations, abiding by the rules of the road, as every upstanding law-abiding citizen should, I pulled my car to a full stop. After looking both ways, as any defensive driver should, I began to proceed through the intersection.

"But as I looked again to my right, I saw a car coming full-bore down the intersecting street. Oftentimes, people will speed up to a stop sign, and then slam on their brakes at the last possible moment. It is often hard to tell if they are going to stop or are going to cruise right on through. Usually, one will make eye contact with the other driver at an intersection, if for no other reason than to nod, indicating that it is all right for you to proceed.

"But the fellow in the approaching car was not making eye contact with me. He was not even looking at me. He had his hand up to the side of his head, engaged in an animated cell phone conversation.

"A little voice in the back of my head screamed at me, *Don't go, don't go*. I immediately removed my foot from the gas pedal. The other car zipped right through the intersection. He did not stop; he did not even slow down. He did not turn his head one way or the other. I do not believe that he even saw me. I do not believe that he saw the stop sign or even realized that there was an intersection there, so involved was he in his telephone conversation. If I had kept my foot on the accelerator, I would have been in the middle of the intersection at the same time that he arrived. I would have been creamed; I would have been toast."

"You would have been creamed toast.

"That's right. My guardian angel had saved me. I breathed a sigh of relief. *Thank you, guardian angel.* That was a close call, as near as a miss can be and still qualify as a miss.

"I would have dismissed the incident as just a close shave, and have been done with it, had not a nearly identical situation happened to me just a short time later that same day. I was approaching another intersection, this time, in front of a mall, where a four-lane roadway abuts the parking lot. As I was cruising along, I noticed a car on one of the exit roads from the parking lot, headed for the four-lane. I had the green light at the time, meaning that the oncoming car had a red light, but it was making no attempt at all to slow down.

"That little voice in the back of my mind screamed out at me again. There was no time to stop, and even if I had applied the brakes, the cars behind me would have turned me into pancake syrup. I cranked the steering wheel hard to the right, went onto the shoulder of the road, and behind the car, as it shot out in front of me. I swear that I could not see daylight between our two vehicles as we passed by a hair's breadth. By some miracle, the other car was able to cross the intersection without colliding with another vehicle. I use the term *miracle*, but in a way, is not the word *miracle* just another way of saying *synchronicity*?

"It only occurred to me as I regained my composure, and my heart went from my mouth back to my chest, that the woman driving the car had failed to observe the light because she was busy talking on her cell phone. The same thing had happened to me twice in the same day. What were the chances of that happening? Certainly strange, but what to make of it?

"Let us put two and two together and see what we come up with. What were the coincident events of the two synchronicities? What are the salient overlapping pieces of the puzzle so that we can connect all the dots?

"First off, I was in a car both times. One similarity. Second similarity: both events occurred at intersections. Third similarity: the drivers were not paying attention, because, fourth similarity: they were talking on cell phones.

"Let us consider the salient points. If these same identical events happened to you, you would be able to add your own personal spin and draw your own conclusions. Remember synchronicities are individual events, intended for the specific individual. To give you an idea of how the meanings of synchronicities may be determined, I will show you how I interpreted this particular one, and how it exactly coincided with the other events that were happening in my life at the moment.

"In the first place, right off the bat, they both happened at intersections. I was driving along the road, and roads have always have that special meaning for me, of moving on, changing course, expanding my horizons.

"The intersections signify a crossroads, where a decision has to be made: *Go straight ahead and continue on the path already embarked upon, or turn one way or the other.* Symbolic, don't you think? Stay tuned. More about this later.

"And, of course, I was in my car. The automobile. Divine symbol of movement, traveling along life's highway, going places. You get the picture."

"Uh huh."

"Next symbol. Both of the cars had nearly hit me because their drivers were talking on cell phones - symbols for communicating.

"And, finally, they were not paying attention. They were ignoring what was around them. They were oblivious to their surroundings.

"So, here is how I put it all together. I was about to make a change in my life. That change involved communicating. Writing a book can certainly be considered communicating. And the book would be about becoming aware of what was all around us: our synchronicities, that we all take for granted."

"And the intersections?"

"Those signify that we are at a crossroads, that as a species, we have reached a critical point in our development. We have a decision to make. Continue on our present self-destructive path, or embark upon a new and glorious adventure of humanity.

"One simple synchronicity. Or just seemingly simple. Do you see how cleverly, how seamlessly the Universe is able to weave many diverse meanings into what might easily have been overlooked? The Universe, in its infinite wisdom, does not waste energy. Why have one meaning when a dozen will do just as well?

"Synchronicities are a constant and ever-present reminder that Creation has a plan, a purpose, a function, a meaning, an intention, a reason, a method to the madness. If the Universe were random chaos, synchronicities would not be possible.

"There you have it, in a nutshell. Do you see how it all fits together?"

She nodded, thinking.

"Let's try another example to illustrate how it works. This one involves numbers. It is, perhaps, one of the most often-seen, or at least, most often-noticed of all the synchronicities. We see numbers, but not just numbers, patterns of numbers.

"The brain tries to make sense of what we experience. Look up into the sky. What do you see? Fluffy white clouds? No, you see a horse, or a rabbit, or a bucking bronco. Patterns that the brain has formed from otherwise amorphous collections of moisture.

"Consider the night sky. Is it filled with pinpoints of light? No, it is occupied by an entire panoply of constellations. Our brain has connected the dots, forming them into dippers and bears and scorpions and lions."

"Lions and tigers and bears."

"Oh, my."

They both laughed.

"So, if a synchronicity stands out, if it is to catch our eye, first and foremost, it must attract our attention," he said. "It must form a pattern.

"How many times do you look at the clock in the course of a day? If you happen to see the numbers read 241, so what? You take no notice of it, because that combination of numbers holds no special significance for you, therefore, you simply disregard it. In order for the synchronicity to draw attention to itself, it must form a pattern."

"I often see 11:11."

"Ah, hah, the infamous eleven eleven. That one jumps out at us. A definite pattern. A highly recognizable form, one that is easy to spot, one that screams out at us to grab our attention."

"What does it mean?"

"Let's analyze it. What could the number eleven mean? It is a classic case of not being able to see the forest for the trees. We see elevens. But what we fail to do is to split it up into its component constituent parts. Not eleven, but one-one. One. The One. The Unit. The Unity. The Singularity. As in single, one. As in Universe. Uni, signifying one. From the Latin unus, meaning one. Oneness. Unity. Anytime we see ones, in whatever pattern, first and foremost, it is a sign that we are all connected, all part of the Eternal One. The Universe. The Oneness. There is a reason why the number one is the first digit in our numbering system.

"Eleven also has a special significance in our culture. The two parallel bars symbolize the parallel dimensions that compose the Universe. It is how the Universe organizes itself into parallel planes of existence.

"Where else do we see the parallel lines of the eleven? The parallel bars of our monetary symbol, the dollar sign. That brings up another interesting point: 911. Watch this."

She leaned over as he wrote 911 it down on the pad. "We start with a nine, then a one and then another one, like this. Now, move the left curve from the top part of the nine and move it upwards. What do you now have? An S. Move the S over the 11 and we have the dollar sign. What buildings were attacked on September Eleventh?"

"The World Trade Center."

"Right. The heart of our financial community. Whenever we see elevens, the Universe is telling us that we are too concerned with monetary matters, i.e., the physical, the material world, and that we need to be concentrating turning our attention to more spiritual concerns. And break the elevens down into their constituent parts, and they are ones. As in *I'm number one, A-number one, look out for number one.*"

"Are you insinuating that I'm greedy, selfish, self-centered?'"

"Don't be insulted; we all suffer from the greed bug. It's catchy."

She crinkled her nose. "I've always heard that when you see your special numbers, that proved that you were spiritual."

He shook his head. "That wouldn't make any sense. There is no such thing as a *go sign*."

"Huh? A *go sign*? What's a *go sign*?"

"Exactly my point. We have stop signs, to warn us that there is imminent danger, but there are on go signs to tell us when to go."

"What about green lights?"

"On a traffic light, which light is the largest?"

She shrugged her shoulders. "I don't know."

"The red light. Which light is on top?"

"Beats me."

"The red light. A traffic light tells us to stop."

"What about when it turns green? It's telling us to go."

"But when our light turns green, it is really a red light for the cross traffic to stop so that they do not collide with us. Our green light is, in actuality, their red light. Like that voice whispering in our ear when we need a nudge, synchronicities are that nudge that we need to send us in the right direction. They show us when we are off track, and need to get back on track. Incidentally, eleven is also the symbol for the parallel train tracks. When we see elevens popping up, we can be sure that the Universe is giving us a gentle nudge to get us back on track."

"So, when we see elevens, we should actually think of ones?"

"Right. All of the various other configurations of elevens, such as 111 or 1111, can be viewed as combinations. But primarily, combinations of ones. The Universe is reminding us that we are connected, part of the Whole, the Oneness, the Unity, and that we need to change our ways in order to manifest that awareness in order to ascend the ladder of spirituality."

"What about other numbers that we might see on a clock?"

"Fair question. In one way of thinking, every number can simply be seen as that number times one. For instance, a seven is seven times one; a five is five times one. And multiplication is merely addition over and over again. So, two is one plus one. And three is one plus one plus one. And four is…"

"I get the idea. That's all the numbers are? Every number is just ones over and over again?"

"Well, the Universe is so omnipotent that it can create multiple symbols, symbols within symbols, so to speak. For example, two, of course, represents the duality of nature. The Yin and Yang, the up and down, left and right, good and evil. Every coin has two sides. Duality is the nature of Universal energy. We cannot have a battery without a positive and a negative pole. Plus and minus. Just as *one* represents the Universe, *two* represents the dichotomy of the Universe. And, of course, 22 is merely 11 times 2. 222 is 111 times 2. And so on and so forth.

"Next comes 333. Three stands for the trinity. In religious terms, the Father, Son, and Holy Ghost. In mathematical terms, the triangle, the golden mean, the three lines of a pyramid's side. Needless to say that 33 is 11 times 3; 333 is 111 times three. Et cetera et cetera.

"Four is twice two, or double duality, so to speak. Duality doubled. All of the larger numbers can be seen as combinations of lower numbers. 5 is 3 plus 2. 6 is 4 plus 2, or 3 plus 3, or two plus two plus two. And the day in Genesis that man was created.

"But, in order to understand any synchronicity, we must consider it in its totality. Not only what the numbers are, but where we see them. After all, the pattern of the numbers is just the vehicle that attracts us to the synchronicity.

"In the above-mentioned case, we are seeing them on the face of the clock. What do clocks signify?"

"Time."

"Right, and all the things that clocks symbolize. For one, we can say that *time is of the essence* and we are misusing it, *that time is running out*, *we are wasting time*. Clock synchronicities in general mean that time is flying and that we had better get cracking and do something. And right now. We do not have a minute to spare, or to lose. The clock is ticking.

"Or, it could mean that we are too controlled by time, always watching the clock, always in a rush to be somewhere, to get something done, to be doing something. Rush, rush, rush. And in our hurry, we are missing the beauty of life, the wonders of the world around us. We should use our time more wisely; slow down and smell the flowers. In our constant mental bedlam, with a million things to do, a billion places to be, we are missing the true meaning of life, the essence of why we are here in the first place. To enjoy life. To appreciate the world that the Universe has bestowed upon us.

"Incidentally, 1111 is seen at the eleventh hour, meaning that we do not have much time to lose. In the common parlance vernacular, *the end is near*.

"Bear in mind that we are only able to see these number synchronicities on the clock because of our modern technology. Years ago, I never once heard anyone say that every time they looked at a clock, the big hand was on the six and the little hand was on the five. It just never happened. But now, I bet that not a day goes by that I do not hear one person or another referring to the odd numbers that keep popping up on the clock. A product of our technology. The very same advanced technology that can doom us can also save us. What a synchronicity!

"If we see the number synchronicities on calendars, it signifies the same thing. A calendar is merely an extended clock. If time is running out in seconds on the clock, then it is running out in days, weeks, months, years, on the calendar.

"Remember, synchronicities are different for each person, and they are particular to the individual. Something that I see whenever I see 1111 are the parallel trunks of trees. What grows on trees? Paper. What is our money? Paper. But also, trees represent life. They purify our atmosphere, recycle the carbon dioxide that we breathe out and give us oxygen to support life. As we destroy our forests, we also put in jeopardy life on this planet. And those trees mean something else - that we can't see the forest for the trees. Remember when I mentioned the bars of eleven-eleven? They mean something else. Those are prison bars."

"Prison? What prison?"

"The prison of our thoughts that we have created and mire us in our own personal hell."

"Wow; that's heavy," she said, contemplating.

He waited for a moment for it to sink in, then continued. "Synchronicities never mean just one thing. Symbols have multiple meanings. The Universe, in its infinite wisdom, never wastes energy, and if it can provide a dozen lessons, or a dozen billion lessons from the same event, then that is exactly what it does. In spades.

"Taken as a whole, synchronicities mean that the Universe is sending us a wake-up call. It is time to get off our duffs, pick ourselves up by our spiritual bootstraps and continue on with our evolution. Our energy is needed elsewhere in the Universe, to be used for other experiments, creating other realities. But it cannot do so if we continue to remain bogged down where we are, immersed in the physical plane of existence. The synchronicity of the clocks is telling us that time is running out, that it is time to move on, to get on with our spiritual development and move up the ladder of human evolution, the next rung of which is the spiritual rung. And, we all have a role to play."

"You keep saying that, but I still don't know how I am supposed to figure out what my role is."

"That's the easy part. Just listen to your inner voice."

"My inner voice? And just how do I hear my inner voice?"

"Glad you asked. If we are a part of the Universe, and we certainly are, then it would stand to reason that connecting with it would be a relatively simple matter, and as it turns out, that is exactly the case.

"All we have to do is rely on that sixth sense, intuition. It goes by many different names - hunches, urges, premonitions, hints, clues, instincts, the voices in our head, as it were. But they are not the bad voices, the voices that drive us insane, telling us to commit evil acts. These are the voices of our inner being speaking to us, communication from our oversoul."

"Oversoul?"

"Our greater self, the source of our being. That inner voice that tells someone not to board a plane that is about to crash, not to step into that elevator that is about to snap its cable, not to step out onto the street into the path of an oncoming car.

"Let us use the example of the plane crash. The plane that we are about to board is going to go down in flames. As physical beings, we have no awareness of that fact. But the Universe knows it full well, and therefore our oversoul knows it also. The thing is, it is not our time to go. Our guardian angel whispers in our ear not to get on the plane. We do not listen. Again, it whispers. Again, we fail to act. So this time, that voice literally screams at us. *Don't get on that plane!* This time, we heed the warning, we change our flight plans at the last minute, and our physical life is spared. It was not our time. We still had things to do, lessons to learn in the physical form. How many times have people been interviewed after a plane crash or some other fatal disaster, and they relate a tale of how they changed their plans at the last minute? And thus, their life was spared. It simply was not their time.

"Such a matter of life and death is, of course, an extreme example. A premonition in such a situation has a profound impact on us. It makes us stand up and take notice. But these same inner hunches occur all the time. You are working on a project that has to be completed by a fast-approaching deadline. You are burning the midnight oil. You pour a cup of coffee to keep yourself awake. As you return to your desk, you set the coffee down. An inner voice tells you not to put it there. You ignore that inner voice; you set the coffee down anyway. Suddenly, the phone rings."

"That's how the phone always rings - suddenly. Especially on a dark and stormy night."

He chuckled. "Right. Automatically, your arm shoots out to pick up the receiver. Your elbow brushes the cup and it spills its contents all over your irreplaceable project. Hours, days, months of work down the drain. Back to the drawing board."

"I hate when that happens."

He nodded. "Here's another example. You are driving down the road."

"I don't drive. I have people for that."

"Please. Humor me."

She smirked. "Consider yourself humored."

"You see a filling station up ahead. That inner voice tells you to pull in and fill up your gas tank. But, you are in a hurry and decide that you will fill it up later. A bit down the road, your car begins to sputter. You look down at the gas gauge and see the needle hovering over the big E. Oops. You should have listened.

"These things happen all the time, since the beginning of time. They are actually more usual than they are unusual. The ancients knew about these messages. They went by various names. Guidance from our inner being, the source of our existence. Our inner spirit, our protector, our guardian angel. Our connection with the Divine Spirit. Our oversoul.

"Whatever we choose to call them, one thing is certain. We ignore them at our peril. They guide us. Help us along the path of life. Point us in the right direction."

"The right direction for what?"

"So that we can do what we are here to do. One thing is certain. The Universe does not waste energy. It would not have created each one of us unless it had a good reason for doing so. Each one of us is a link in the chain of life. Remove a link and the chain collapses. The chain cannot exist without the links. Each of the links is as important as any of the other links. No one link is any more, or less, important than any of the others. The chain only works when all of the links are working together, in unison. As a unit. A complete whole. People call it a *chain*, not a collection of individual links.

"In the vast scheme of things, we are all links in the chain, working together in a cooperative effort. Each one of those links has a purpose, a reason for being here. Without any one of those links, the chain would not be as complete as it is.

"When we speak of a chain, it is easy to see the purpose of each individual link. When we look at our own existence, it is sometimes more difficult to see exactly why it is that we are here.

"But our oversoul knows. The source of our being knows exactly what we are supposed to be doing here, why we entered the physical realm in the first place. We often lament, *if only the Universe would tell us why we are here*.

"As it turns out, it does just exactly that. We receive messages from our oversoul all the time. But we often do not hear them because there is so much going on in our heads, the constant clatter of mental clutter: *Pick up a loaf of bread on the way home from work, get the assignment done by Wednesday, take Junior to soccer practice*, and on and on and on. Our lives are so full of things to do, places to go, people to meet, that the voices in our heads begin to resemble a cacophony."

"If there is so much going on in our heads that we cannot even hear our own selves think, then what chance do we have of ever hearing our higher spirits speaking to us?" she asked.

"The key is to silence the extraneous noises in our head so that we can hear our inner voice. If we are receiving messages from the Infinite, then there must be a reason. And the Universe would not send a message unless it intended us to hear. We have no problem hearing these in a life-and-death situation."

"If only our guardian angels spoke to us as forcefully all the time, to give us inner guidance, show us the path of life we should be taking, that life would be so much easier."

"The fact of the matter is, our inner self does speak to us constantly. Since we are intimately connected with the source of our being, we are in constant communication. We only have to make the effort, and take the time to listen. All it involves is refocusing our attention.

"Try this experiment the next time you are in a crowded room. When you first enter a party, with wall-to-wall people, each group carrying on their separate conversation, it is a loud din. At first, you cannot make out what anyone is saying. You join a group and tune into their conversation. Suddenly, you can understand them perfectly, and all of the other conversations in the room fade into the background murmur. When you move from that group to another, you tune in on their conversation, blocking the others out. You only hear the conversation of the group that you are concentrating on.

"You can do the same thing at a restaurant or dinner party. You can easily carry on a conversation with the person sitting next to you, then redirect your concentration to the person on the other side of you or across the table, directing your conversation, as it were, to those specific people, sending the others into the hiss of background clamor. Even though there might be many conversations going on in the room at the same time, the only one you hear is the one you are concentrating on. In fact, if you are deeply absorbed in the interesting conversation going on at your table, you might be completely oblivious to all the others going on in the room simultaneously.

"Our brain serves the same function, focusing our attention in the physical plane and blocking out all the information we receive from other realms of existence. That information is there, at our disposal, to be used whenever the spirit moves us, but we only tune in to it on those rare occasions. We often get mental glimpses of it, but usually choose to ignore it, just as we ignore all of those other conversations going on in the room around us."

"How then, can we hear those hidden messages?"

"We are connected with the Infinite. All we have to do is tune in to it. There is a constant interplay, a communication, but most of the time our brain filters it out. All we have to do to communicate with the Infinite is to still the multitudinous voices in our mind and tune in to the messages we wish to hear.

"This involves stilling the mind. It is a process that many seers and mystics have used over the years. It is a favorite of the yogis. It is, of course, meditation.

"Although the technique has long been popular with Eastern mystics, it did not enter the Western vogue until the late sixties, when it was popularized by the *Beatles*. They traveled to India and studied with the Maharishi Mahesh Yogi, in order to gain enlightenment, inner peace, and tranquility. This is what *Transcendental Meditation*, or *TM*, as it is popularly called, promised. Calming the mind brought endless bliss to the human body.

"The yogis learned this through years of practice, many hours a day. The yogi is able to control functions of the autonomic nervous system that Western science previously considered beyond the range of conscious control. For instance, the yogis can actually regulate their heart rate, as well as their blood pressure and temperature. They are able to clear their minds completely of any image or idea whatsoever, creating a blank slate, as it were.

"This is a difficult trick to learn. Try to think of absolutely nothing for the next ten minutes. Go ahead, do it now."

She closed her eyes. The strained expression on her face indicated that she was concentrating intensely. After a moment, she re-opened her eyes, obviously frustrated.

"You cannot do it, can you? Thoughts immediately come rushing into your consciousness. All the things that need to be done, should be done, undoubtedly won't get done. That is the nature of the beast. Our mind is so preoccupied with so many things that it simply refuses to be stilled."

"How can we clear our mind of all thoughts, then?"

"We could leave our happy home and go live in the Himalaya Mountains of Tibet and study with the yogis. A few dozen years should do the trick to be able to achieve peace and contentment."

"Who has the time? There must be a better way."

"Not better or worse, just different. Remember, we can sometimes hear those inner voices. So, we know already that they are there. All we need to do is to be able to hear them at will, on a more regular basis.

"As it turns out, the Universe, in its infinite wisdom, has provided an easy answer. You did not think that it would be hard, did you? The trick is to clear the mind so that the messages we wish to hear can come through."

"But how do we completely still the mind?"

"As it turns out, when we are entertaining a thought, that thought pushes the others out. Try this little exercise. Try to think of two songs at the same time; try to hum one and think of another."

She gave it her best effort, to no avail.

"You cannot do it, can you? Our brain is like a one-track mind. It can only concentrate on one thing at a time. I am not referring to multi-tasking, where you walk and chew gum at the same time. I am referring to entertaining two completely disparate ideas in our mind simultaneously, like reciting a poem and doing the multiplication tables at once. Or performing two completely different songs, in different keys and tempos, on the piano with both hands at the same time. Unless you are bilateral and ambidextrous, you cannot do it, and if you can, then you are obviously far beyond anything I could ever teach you.

"So, if the brain is a one-track mind, then the thing to do is to occupy our brain in such a way that we entertain one thought and force the others out the back door of the mind. This is focused attention, or meditation, or heightened concentration, or relaxation technique. We think of one thing, to the exclusion of all others. While we have that thought firmly in place, nothing else can enter to distract us. In effect, we have shut out all of the mental noise running through our mind so that we can finally hear ourselves think."

"And just how are you supposed to do that?"

"There are a number of ways. It all involves concentration, focusing our attention on one thing, to the exclusion of all others.

"Here is how it is done. Stretch out and lie still."

She did as he instructed.

"You can be lying down or stretched out in an easy chair. The point is to assume a relaxed position so that there is no stress on the body. It might help to loosen your belt and remove your shoes."

Again, she followed his instructions.

"It depends on the time and place, of course, but the idea is to select a comfortable position. Some people have found success in monitoring their breathing. Normally, we take our breathing for granted. The air crawls in, the air crawls out. It has become so automatic that we rarely even give it a thought, until that is, our air passages are constricted by a cold or we are under water, and we suddenly become acutely aware of our breathing. Concentrate on your breathing, on your diaphragm going up and down, of your chest rising and falling. In out, in out, in out. This focuses the attention and removes the noise in our head.

"Another way of accomplishing the same thing is to think of a calming situation. Perhaps you enjoy the beach. You find yourself calm and relaxed watching the waves lap up upon the shore. Picture that image in your mind. The waves breaking on the sand. As you concentrate on this picture in your mind, you will begin to feel calm and relaxed.

"Alternatively, you can create an image in your mind of a bank of clouds overhead. Or the wind gently blowing through a field of grain, whipping the stalks from side to side. A calm, relaxing image.

"You can employ whatever image you find calming and relaxing. It does not matter what it is, as long as it works for you.

"There is another simple technique that is easily learned, in fact, do it one time and you will be an expert. It involves concentrating on your body, and feeling each part, each joint, each nerve becoming calm and relaxed. I will walk you through it. Of course, I will say the affirmations out loud, but the idea for you is to repeat them silently, to yourself. By speaking to yourself, you will come to learn the sound of your inner voice, and thus, you will be able to recognize the Universal voice when it speaks to you.

"Start off with your toes and work your way up the body. Use the names for the parts of the body that you are familiar and comfortable with. I'll give you an example just to get you started. I'll say the words out loud; you repeat them to yourself silently. Now, let's begin."

He began speaking in a calm, soft voice, reciting the following affirmations:

My toes are calm and relaxed.
My toes are calm and relaxed.
My toes are calm and relaxed.

My heels are calm and relaxed.
My heels are calm and relaxed.
My heels are calm and relaxed.

My feet are calm and relaxed.
My feet are calm and relaxed.
My feet are calm and relaxed.

My ankles are calm and relaxed.
My ankles are calm and relaxed.
My ankles are calm and relaxed.

My shins are calm and relaxed.
My shins are calm and relaxed.
My shins are calm and relaxed.

My knees are calm and relaxed.
My knees are calm and relaxed.
My knees are calm and relaxed.

My thighs are calm and relaxed.
My thighs are calm and relaxed.
My thighs are calm and relaxed.

My pelvis is calm and relaxed.
My pelvis is calm and relaxed.
My pelvis is calm and relaxed.

My seat is calm and relaxed.
My seat is calm and relaxed.
My seat is calm and relaxed.

My stomach is calm and relaxed.
My stomach is calm and relaxed.
My stomach is calm and relaxed.

My chest is calm and relaxed.
My chest is calm and relaxed.
My chest is calm and relaxed.

My back is calm and relaxed.
My back is calm and relaxed.
My back is calm and relaxed.

My spine is calm and relaxed.
My spine is calm and relaxed.
My spine is calm and relaxed.

2012

My fingers are calm and relaxed.
My fingers are calm and relaxed.
My fingers are calm and relaxed.

My wrists are calm and relaxed.
My wrists are calm and relaxed.
My wrists are calm and relaxed.

My forearms are calm and relaxed.
My forearms are calm and relaxed.
My forearms are calm and relaxed.

My elbows are calm and relaxed.
My elbows are calm and relaxed.
My elbows are calm and relaxed.

My biceps are calm and relaxed.
My biceps are calm and relaxed.
My biceps are calm and relaxed.

My shoulders are calm and relaxed.
My shoulders are calm and relaxed.
My shoulders are calm and relaxed.

My neck is calm and relaxed.
My neck is calm and relaxed.
My neck is calm and relaxed.

My chin is calm and relaxed.
My chin is calm and relaxed.
My chin is calm and relaxed.

2012

My lips are calm and relaxed.
My lips are calm and relaxed.
My lips are calm and relaxed.

My nose is calm and relaxed.
My nose is calm and relaxed.
My nose is calm and relaxed.

My cheeks are calm and relaxed.
My cheeks are calm and relaxed.
My cheeks are calm and relaxed.

My ears are calm and relaxed.
My ears are calm and relaxed.
My ears are calm and relaxed.

My eyes are calm and relaxed.
My eyes are calm and relaxed.
My eyes are calm and relaxed.

My forehead is calm and relaxed.
My forehead is calm and relaxed.
My forehead is calm and relaxed.

My head is calm and relaxed.
My head is calm and relaxed.
My head is calm and relaxed.

My whole body is calm and relaxed.
My whole body is calm and relaxed.
My whole body is calm and relaxed.

Om.
Om.
Om.

He continued, "When I open my eyes, my entire being will be calm and relaxed. I will be totally awake, alert, but feeling totally at peace, calm and relaxed, bathed in the infinite bliss of the Universe."

She opened her eyes, rolled them back and forth, grinned.

"How do you feel?" he asked.

"Calm and relaxed." She smiled. "Groovy. What's that *um* business about?"

"Not um; om. That's a mantra, a sound that is repeated to focus the mind during meditation. Om is the sacred sound of the Universe. The music of the spheres. Like it?"

"Uh uhm."

"And bear in mind that this first session was just an example to get you started. Once you get comfortable with it, feel free to change it in any way that feels comfortable to you. For example, the terms that I used for the body parts are my words; you can use any words you like."

"How much is enough? How long am I supposed to meditate?"

"That's the first question the new meditator always asks, *How long should I meditate?* You might as well ask, *How much water should I drink?* The answer to both is the same: Your body will tell you. Unerringly. Under normal circumstances, the body knows just how much liquid you need. It is called *thirst*. When you become thirsty, you drink a glass of water or other fluid. When your thirst is quenched, you stop drinking. No one has to tell you how much is enough. You just automatically know.

"Joggers will tell you the same thing. How far should one jog? On some days, one feels drained after a hard day at the salt mine, and might feel like jogging for many miles to relieve the stress; at other times, a shorter distance will suffice. It is an innate feeling, inherent in the body. Your body will tell you when enough is enough; learn to listen to it. Like drinking water, or jogging, after a while, you will just know."

"That doesn't tell me much."

"As a general rule of thumb, it takes ten or fifteen minutes for the mind to become relaxed. You can feel the stress and anxiety drifting away from your body, becoming calm and relaxed. Your brain waves slow down, and a sense of relaxed euphoria sweeps over your body. Once you feel it, you will know what I mean. The tension just drifts away, your entire body feels calm and relaxed. Your brain glides on an ocean of tranquility.

"How long would you sleep at night? An hour? Ten hours? Twenty? Twenty-four? No one needs to tell you how long to sleep, or when you need sleep, for that matter. When your body is rested, you wake up. It comes naturally. Unless, of course, the alarm clock wrests you from your slumbers, but that is another story entirely."

She groaned. "Alarm clocks should be banned. There ought to be a law."

He nodded agreement. "With sleep, each person has their own demands, which can vary from day to day, depending on the amount of stress you are under, among other things. At times, five hours of sleep will suffice, and at other times, ten hours will not seem nearly enough.

"The same goes for meditation. It is an individual thing. Some people need more, some need less. Ten, fifteen, twenty minutes are sufficient to lower your brain waves. Two sessions a day, fifteen or twenty minute each, should be more than adequate. But in the final analysis, those are just guidelines. Like drinking water or jogging or sleeping, the real answer is, whatever feels right for you. You be the judge. Your body will tell you if you need more.

"But make sure you do it every day. When you are learning to play an instrument, your instructor might tell you to practice an hour a day. A little at a time. Practice makes perfect. You cannot save it up, intending to practice for seven hours on Sunday. It doesn't work that way.

"Meditation is the same. A little goes a long way. Shorter sessions, every day produces better results than marathon infrequent sessions. And I repeated each affirmation three times, but you can do as many times as you like. You can do them five times or ten times, or go through the same process several times, from start to finish; it's up to you. Let your consciousness be your guide. It will steer you unerringly along the right path."

She pondered for a moment, taking in all that he had said. "And doing that, meditating, will change the world for the better?"

"Be making yourself calmer and more relaxed, you automatically lower the fear and anxiety level of the planetary consciousness. That reduces the negative energy, making the world a better place."

"Come on; give me a break. What can one person do?"

"People often ask, *what difference can one person make in the vast scheme of things*? Well, as we found out in the Presidential election of 2000, one person can indeed make a great deal of difference. The election was decided by a mere handful of voters. People do not realize how truly powerful they are, or the impact they have on the world. One person can make a big difference.

"Each day, we come into contact with many people. We make our mark, leave an impression on them all. Remember, there is only one person we can change in this world, and that is the person in the mirror.

"We can change ourselves, and collectively, we can change the world. As we change, by definition, so does the Universe. As we grow and learn, the Universe grows and learns."

"And meditation can do all that?" she asked.

"Meditation is only half of the equation. Meditation is the mental process; the thought. We reinforce the thought with an action. A prayer action."

"A prayer is an action? You lost me there."

He chuckled. "Let me find you again. Do you remember when I mentioned the *collective unconscious*?"

"Vaguely."

"Well, it's the consciousness shared by all human beings on the face of the planet. But, humans aren't the only consciousnesses on the planet. The planet itself, along with everything that's on it, every animal, every plant, every insect, every bird, every tree, every creature…"

"Every rock?"

He nodded sagely. "Yes, even every rock, they all form a closed system, a collective mass of consciousness, if you will. For the sake of discussion, let's just call it the *planetary consciousness*. When you meditate, you lower the negative energy of the planetary consciousness. That's half the battle. The other half is raising the positive energy. You might think of it as a seesaw; you know, a teeter totter."

"I know what a seesaw is."

"Well, think of a seesaw, with good on one side and evil on the other."

"Evil being the eight-hundred pound gorilla, no doubt."

"No doubt." He chuckled. "That is a good analogy. Evil is an eight-hundred pound gorilla. That should give you some idea which side that scale is tipped."

"You got that right."

"At any rate, at the present moment, the seesaw is tipped far to the side of Evil. And that is especially dangerous at this point in our history. We have nuclear devices that could obliterate the planet, and chemical and biological agents that could very well reduce the population to zero. The stakes have never been higher."

"So, we should prayer for peace?"

"Yes and no."

"Yes and no? What sense does that make?"

"Yes, in the sense that we should pray for peace; but no in the sense that we should pray for peace."

"Now, you've really got me really confused."

"You hit the nail right smack dab on the head. The fact of the matter is, most people are confused about prayer. This will take a little bit of explaining; this is tricky, so bear with me.

"Let's say that someone looks around them and all they see is evil, evil everywhere. So they say to themselves, self, there is so much evil in this world that I must pray for peace. Now, I'm going to use a little stretch of the imagination here. Let's say that the person in question is going to pray one hundred prayer units."

"What's that?"

"No idea. It's just a convenient number to add and subtract. Stay with me here."

"I'm with you. All the way."

"Okay. Good. Now, the person has one hundred units of prayer. But remember, when they surveyed the world, they said that there was so much evil, they needed to pray for peace. A portion of their consciousness is focused on the evil in the world. So, instead of devoting the full one hundred prayer units for peace, let's say that forty consciousness units are focused on evil and only sixty prayer units actually get focused on peace. So, the forty evil units water down the sixty good units, and the net result is that only twenty units are directed toward positive energy. Does that make sense?"

"Sure, the evil thoughts cancel out the good thoughts."

"Exactly. We're praying with one hundred units of prayer, but only twenty of them actually are directed toward positive energy."

"Got you. You're using a hundred prayer units, but only twenty are actually doing any good."

"Hey, you catch no fast."

She beamed. "I'm a quick study."

"The thing is, people think when they pray that they are investing the full force of their prayer energy toward accomplishing good, when in fact, the truth of the matter is that only a portion of that total prayer energy ever accomplishes anything. One part of the brain is focused on the evil and it dilutes the positive prayer energy, so it has less of an effect. As a matter of fact, it can actually work the other way. Let's say that you believe so much in evil that it is constantly on your mind. When you pray for good, half of your mind is concentrated on all the evil in the world and the other half is praying for peace. They cancel each other out. Net result, zero."

"Or, even worse, say that you are so concerned with evil that your hundred prayer units are divided sixty for evil and only forty for good. In that case, you actually have a net negative result. I know it sounds absurd, but that is exactly what happens. That is why, the harder we want something, and the harder we try to get it, our effort can actually become counter-productive, because so much of our energy is focused on the fact that we don't have it, and those thoughts of deficiency completely negate the positive energy that we are trying to produce."

"So, the more we try, the worse the results."

"Right. The harder you try, the harder it becomes to achieve your objective, because the harder you try, the more negative energy you generate, which serves to counteract the results you are trying to achieve, and your success becomes that much more elusive. We just have to release it, let it go, and then, we can get what we're after, because we're not canceling out the positive energy."

"So, if we pray for peace, we don't get peace?"

"No; that's not exactly what I mean."

"What do you mean?"

"What I'm saying is, our prayers are not as effective as they could be, because we're concentrating a portion of our energy on the opposite effect. In other words, we see evil; we acknowledge it. We pray for peace, our infamous hundred prayer units. But since forty-five of those units are concentrated on evil, only fifty-five units are concentrated on peace, and we end up with only ten positive prayer units.

"And then, there's another question. What do you pray for?"

"We pray for what's best for us, naturally."

"What is best for us? We never seem to know. And it keeps changing. Our friends become our enemies and our enemies become our friends. Our allies in the First World War became our enemies in the Second World War and vice versa. The guerillas that we supported have turned into the terrorists who attack us. The thing is, we really don't know what to pray for, because we don't have the perspective to see the bigger picture; we never know how things are going to turn out. We may think that we're doing something that is really good, when in fact, it could turn out to be the worst possible thing somewhere down the line."

She contemplated. "I know; we could just pray for the *greatest good* and let God decide what that is."

"Hmmm. It's a good intention. Your heart's in the right place, but you still are missing the point. Maybe I can illustrate it with a story. Remember when you were a kid? Let's say that you wanted a new bicycle for Christmas."

"I did, once."

"Did you pray for it?"

"Lots."

"Hmmm." He scratched his chin. "That brings up another interesting point. I'll get back to that in a minute. But first, did you get the bike?"

"Finally." She sighed.

"Once you got the bicycle, did you continue to pray for it?"

"Of course not. That would be silly. Why would I do that when I already had it?"

"Exactly my point."

"Huh? What is your point?"

"The point is, you only pray when you think that you need to pray."

"Well, duh." She snapped her gum.

"So, you said that you would pray for the greatest good, thinking that would eliminate any negative energy entirely. But, you only pray for something when you think that you don't have it. You only prayed for the bicycle when you didn't have it. So, when you pray for the greatest good, part of your brain is saying, the world is full of rage and hatred and anger and envy and greed and all sorts of evil. So, to counteract that, you're going to pray for the greatest good. But the fact remains, if you actually thought that the world were full of peace and goodness and justice and kindness and compassion, you wouldn't bother to pray at all, because you already had what you were praying for. Think about it. You only prayed for the bicycle when you didn't have it. So, by the same token, you only pray for the greatest good when you are convinced that the world is filled with the greatest evil."

"So, even then, you're diluting your prayer power."

"Exactly."

"So, what do we pray for?"

"What we have to do is change our method of prayer completely. The whole way that we pray is really askew. Remember when you wanted the bicycle? You prayed for days, weeks, maybe even months. And then, on Christmas morning, you looked under the tree and there it was, your nice new bicycle, with a big bow. So, what did you do?"

"Hopped right on it."

"Right. The first thing you did was climbed aboard and road off. But remember, you had been praying for months for that bike. Now that you had it, how long did you say a prayer of *thank you* for your new bike? Maybe once? Maybe a single prayer at bedtime? *Thanks for the bike*, and you crawled under the covers and fell asleep and that was the end of your appreciation. Does that seem like any sort of psychic balance?"

"Well, now that you mention it..."

"Our prayers are always *gimme gimme gimme*. They're rarely ever *thank you thank you thank you*. And that, in and of itself, creates a psychic imbalance in the planetary consciousness.

"What we have to do is turn our demands into thankfulness; show some appreciation for all that we have. Each morning, as soon as we open our eyes, we should start our day with a great big *thank-you* to the

Universe for giving us another day, for the air we breathe, for the food we eat, for the roof over our head, for the clothes on our back, and just to be alive, in general. We have so much to be thankful for. We have to adopt an attitude of gratitude. The positive energy that that creates will spill out into our daily lives and affect in a positive manner everyone we come in contact with.

"And therein lies the key to generating positive prayer energy. By giving back."

"Giving back what? To whom?"

"To the Universe. We wonder why we are here, what we are supposed to do, or rather, what can the Universe do for us? We need to turn that sentiment around. To paraphrase a famous leader, *ask not what your Universe can do for you; ask what you can do for your Universe.*"

"And how do we do that?"

"By performing Acts of Planetary Kindness."

"What's that?"

"You might call it a prayer with a hundred percent positive energy attached. Remember the seesaw effect? You saw evil all around, so you prayed for peace? In that case, the energy attached to the negative thought cancels out some of the positive energy. When you perform an APK, you don't even think of the negative. You only think in terms of doing something good for the planetary consciousness. That way, you have all of the positive energy without any of the negative ramifications."

"Give me a for instance." She snapped her gum.

"Okay." He thought. "You chew gum."

"It relaxes me." Snap. Snap.

"You open the wrapper, pop the gum into your mouth, and unconsciously you toss the wrapper on the floor."

"Oh, it's not unconscious at all; I do it on purpose."

"You do?" he asked, flabbergasted.

"Sure; that's what the floor is there for - to catch things."

"But, it makes a mess."

"That's what I have people for. To unmess the messes I create."

"Everyone doesn't have assistants."

"I keep forgetting. I just take it for granted that everyone has people to pick up after them."

"Everyone isn't famous like you."

"Well, duh."

"At any rate, the next time you chew a stick of gum, instead of casually tossing the wrapper away, place it in a trash receptacle. If there is no trash can around, then put it in your pocket until you come to a waste basket."

"Why would I do that?"

"It's giving back to the Planetary Consciousness. Do not do it with the idea that the world is a dirty place and you have to clean it up. That would only add negative energy to the system. Do it simply with the thought that the Universe has given you bountiful riches, and you are giving back some of those blessings. It is a simple act, but many such acts, repeated over the course of a month, a year, a lifetime, by many similar people, will have profound effects.

"Let me try another example. You know all those abandoned carts in the parking lot at the grocery store?"

"Yeah."

"Well, the next time you go shopping, just push one of those carts into the store and use it. That way, you eliminated a cart that cars have to maneuver around, and you saved someone the bother of collecting one more cart."

She smacked her gum. "I never shop."

"Do you eat?"

"Sure, but I have people who shop for me."

"You're missing the point."

"Obviously. What is the point?"

"The point is to do a simple Act of Planetary Kindness each and every day. It doesn't have to be a big thing; it can be a small thing." He thought. "Like giving a sandwich to a homeless person."

"Oh, ugh. I would never go near a homeless person."

"Why not?"

"Because, duh, they're homeless."

"Do you ever do anything for yourself?"

"Of course not; that's what I have people for." She suddenly beamed. "I know; I can have my people do it for me. Every day, I'll have one of them do something nice for the planet." She snapped her gum. Twice.

His eyes began to cross.

"And then," she said, "they'll give me an award and I'll get all kinds of free publicity." She smiled. "Hey, this good-deed doing might not be such a bad deal after all."

"No! that's the last thing you want to do. Keep it to yourself. If you brag about it, if you even mention it, you are doing it for the wrong reason, not for altruistic ends, but for selfish motives of acclaim and fame and recognition. If you even mention the act, you diminish the effect; negate it. The negative energy contravenes the positive energy and cancels out the good effects. You can even end up with a net loss of energy. I cannot emphasize that strongly enough; do not, I repeat, do not reveal to anyone the kindness that you have done. Keep it under your hat."

"You mean, light a candle, and then hide it under my hat?"

"Exactly."

"Why do something if you don't get credit for it? What's the point? That makes no sense at all."

"It makes perfect sense. In this case, silence is indeed golden. Broadcasting your good deed only serves to dilute the effort and thwart the effect, because, in that case, it is being done for the wrong reasons, to heap glory on oneself. Instead of an act of planetary kindness, it becomes a self-serving act, or even worse, it becomes a competition, trying to outdo the next guy. For instance, consider the following typical exchange between two planetary kindnessers who happen to bump into each other on the street." He located a sheet of paper which contained the following:

EXT. BUSY STREET - DAY
Two acquaintances, going in opposite directions, bump into each other.

                          Person A
Hello, Person B, how is your day going?

                          Person B
Good. I just performed an act of planetary kindness. Feel free to pat me on the back.

                          Person A
Oh, really. I never took you for one of *those*. What did you do?

                          Person B
I did X. Go ahead; pat me on the back; I deserve it. After all, I am a superior individual, worthy of your admiration, praise, and high accolades.

                          Person A
You think what you did was so great? So what? I can top that. I'll have you know that I did X, plus one percent. So, there; I deserve a pat on the back, plus one percent.

                          Person B
Oh yeah? Well I can top that. I did double X. So, I deserve a double pat on the back.

                          Person A
Oh yeah, well I did double X, plus one percent, so I deserve a double pat on the back, plus one percent.

Alpha Omega inserted the paper between the pages of his *Bible*. "That's as far as I got, but I think you can see where this is going. I will spare you the gory details of the fist fight that ensued."

She laughed. "I can imagine."

"When we do good things for the wrong reasons, we add negativity to the mix, and our negative energy dilutes, if not totally negates, the positive effects."

He opened his *Bible* to Matthew 6:1 and read: *Take heed that ye do not your alms before men, to be seen of them: otherwise ye have no reward of your Father which is in heaven. Therefore when thou doest thine alms, do not sound a trumpet before thee, as the hypocrites do in the synagogues and in the streets, that they may have glory of men.*

"He ran his finger down to Matthew 6:3, and continued reading: *But when thou doest alms, let not thy left hand know what thy right hand doeth: that thine alms may be in secret.*

He pulled the sheet of paper out of the *Bible* and turned it over. "Now, let us revisit the chance meeting on the street of our illustrious Person A and Person B. But this time, you will notice that they keep their Acts of Planetary Kindness to themselves."

EXT. BUSY STREET - DAY
Two acquaintances, going in opposite directions, bump into each other.

Person A
Hello, Person B, how is your day going?

Person B
Good.
(Notice that Person B neglected to mention any Act of Planetary Kindness.)

Person A

Good? Only Good!? That's nothing. I can top that. Let me tell you, my day is going great!

Person B

Oh yeah? Well, my day is going better than great; my day is going great, plus one percent!

Person A

So what? My day is going great plus two percent!

Person B

Oh yeah, well my day is going double great!!

Person A

That's nothing. My day is going double great plus one percent!!!

"Once again," Alpha said, "I will spare you the gory details of the fist fight that climaxed their otherwise *great* day, but I am sure you get the general idea. It is not only what we do, but how we do it, and with what intentions. Actions speak louder than words, so therefore, we should perform our Acts of Planetary Kindness in silence.

"Everyone is searching for the proverbial magic bullet. As it turns out, it is not magic at all; it's only three simple things - we, ourselves, and us. If we change our attitude, our thoughts, then we change the world. Calming and relaxing ourselves through meditation, performing daily Acts of Planetary Kindness, using our synchronicities to guide us on the path of our earthly mission, by doing these things, we live up to our potential and maximize the potential of the planet.

"This has never been more important than it is at this point in our history. Our modern technology is a two-edged sword. It holds our future, but it can also hold the seeds of our own destruction.

2012

"We live in a time of global communication. Cable, worldwide television, and the internet connect every corner of the globe. But, not only do they spread information, they also spread fear and panic. The instant access to information keeps us up-to-date and informed, but it also keeps us anxious and fearful. That negative energy of fear and anxiety becomes a self-fulfilling prophecy. We were fearful of the arrival of Y2K, fearing the worst would happen, and voila, we got what we feared. The snowball effect of that fear produced the Stock Market collapse, the dot com implosion, and even the September Attacks, as well as an influx of global weather cataclysms, a rise of exotic diseases, and a whole host of other *natural* disasters. *Natural*, not in the sense of *acts of God*, but *natural* in the sense that *we* caused them.

"We are our own worst enemy. An old adage goes: *Be careful of what you wish for; you may get it*. In this modern age of mass media, that adage needs to be updated - *Be careful of what you fear; it will become your reality*.

"On the other hand, by meditating and performing daily Acts of Planetary Kindness, we bathe the world in positive energy and then people automatically make better decisions in their daily lives. We create a mental atmosphere that's more conducive to positive effects. So, when someone is faced with the decision to strap a bomb on themselves and blow themselves up, along with a hundred other people, they make the right decision, and say, *No, I'm not going to do that*. Or when terrorists are given the choice to fly a plane into a building, they say, *No thank you, not today, we'll pass on that*. Or when a mother is confronted with the choice of either drowning her children or seeking help, she will make the proper decision."

"And just by thinking good thoughts, we're going to accomplish all that?" she asked, with a doubtful twist to her grin.

He smiled. "How do you feel on a bright, sunny day?"

"Wonderful."

"Exactly. You feel better, so you behave better, you treat other people better. And on a dull gloomy overcast day, you feel cranky and out of sorts. You feel miserable and consequently, you treat people miserably."

She was not convinced. "This stuff all sounds like... well, to put it bluntly, a little Pollyanna-ish to me. You really believe that just by thinking good thoughts and doing a good deed every day that you can actually change the world?"

"Who's to say? Anyway, isn't it worth a try? Ever heard of *Pascal's wager?*"

She thought for a moment. "Sure; Jimmy Pascal, the bass player for the rock group, *Death and Destruction.*"

He laughed. "Not hardly. Blaise Pascal was a Seventeenth Century philosopher. What he said, in a nutshell, was, if you believe in God, and live your life accordingly, then when you die, if you're wrong, you haven't lost much at all, but if you're right, then you have gained a great deal. So, just being logical and prudent, there is only one sensible way to comport one's life.

"The same holds true in this case. Basically, we have nothing to lose and everything to gain."

She pondered. "Maybe so, but still, the whole thing sounds a little far-fetched to me."

He settled back, staring off into space, his lips parted in an inscrutable smile. "How will we know until we try?"

The End

2012

Quirigua Stele C

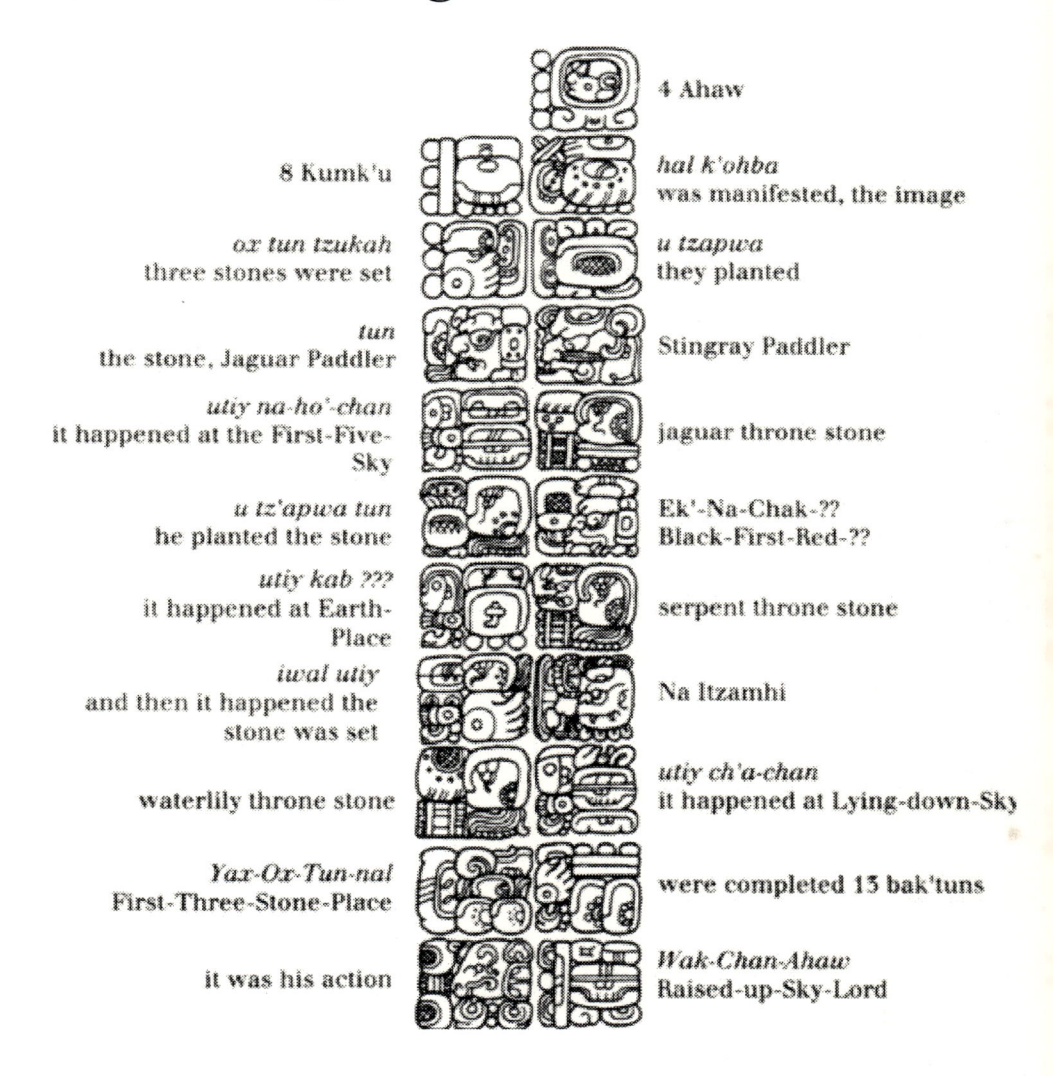

	4 Ahaw
8 Kumk'u	hal k'ohba was manifested, the image
ox tun tzukah three stones were set	u tzapwa they planted
tun the stone, Jaguar Paddler	Stingray Paddler
utiy na-ho'-chan it happened at the First-Five-Sky	jaguar throne stone
u tz'apwa tun he planted the stone	Ek'-Na-Chak-?? Black-First-Red-??
utiy kab ??? it happened at Earth-Place	serpent throne stone
iwal utiy and then it happened the stone was set	Na Itzamhi
waterlily throne stone	utiy ch'a-chan it happened at Lying-down-Sky
Yax-Ox-Tun-nal First-Three-Stone-Place	were completed 13 bak'tuns
it was his action	Wak-Chan-Ahaw Raised-up-Sky-Lord

Graphic from: *Maya Cosmos* by David Freidel, Linda Schele, and Joy Parker. Used with permission.